CW00688308

TERRY ABRAHAM
LIFE ON THE MOUNTAINS

DEDICATED TO MY WIFE SUE,
AND IN LOVING MEMORY OF
HERBERT AND LYDIA ABRAHAM

Credits

Written by Terry Abraham © May 2020.
As told to John Manning.
All photos © Terry Abraham, except p. 17, p. 133 © Nathan Buckley, p. 129 © Andrew Locking, p. 135 © David Forster and back cover © Paul Bacon.
Design by Andrew Chapman / www.chapmandesign.net
Proofread by Georgia Laval.

Printed by Latitude.

SBN 978-1-9998940-6-1
A catalogue for this book is available from the British Library.
All rights reserved.

No part of this publication may be reproduced, stored in retrieval systems or transmitted in any form or by any means, electronic, mechanical, photocopying, recording or otherwise without the prior written permission of the publisher and copyright holder.

Terry can be found on Twitter @terrybnd and on Facebook Terry Abraham - Outdoors Filmmaker and Photographer

Published May 2020 by Jake Island Ltd, 3 Brunt How, Loughrigg, Cumbria LA22 9HE.

Terry Abraham: Life on the Mountains is an Inspired by Lakeland title.

For news and other publications see inspiredbylakeland.co.uk.
To get in touch email hello@inspiredbylakeland.co.uk

Printed on woodland-friendly FSC stock.

FOREWORDS

◄
Autumnal sunset: 'Red screes' and the Scafells.

ERIC ROBSON

This splendid book is the perfect introduction to the great mountains of Lakeland. Yet it came about by accident. Author Terry Abraham was made redundant from his job in IT and suddenly had the time and space to explore the mountains in the footsteps of his hero Alfred Wainwright.

While AW recorded the spectacle in pen and ink, Terry would eventually capture the scene on state-of-the-art cameras and recorders. But however different their method, they both knew that to do the scenes justice they had to have a grasp of geology and geography, history and botany. They also had to capture the fact that these were and still are working landscapes, making their living from a combination of tourism and farming.

There's a refreshing lack of experts in Terry's films. Local people are allowed to speak for themselves and invite us into their traditional gatherings, such as their valley shows and shepherds' meets.

Terry's *Life of a Mountain* trilogy is graced by exquisite photography, much of it helped by Terry's fondness for wild camping. At the going down of the sun and in the morning he would be ahead of the game, waiting for the perfectly framed sunset or the first flash of morning glory.

Even though I know Scafell and Blencathra and Helvellyn well, there are captured landscapes in these films and this book that I've never seen. This book is a stunning contribution to Lakeland literature and I can't recommend it highly enough.

STUART MACONIE

Lakes Poets don't always come in frock coats from Cockermouth and Hawkshead. Sometimes they come from the East Midlands, wear hiking sandals and drink beer. They don't always wander lonely as a cloud, either. Sometimes they wander with a sound recordist and a drone pilot and the occasional anxious writer/broadcaster in tow. I know, for I've been that last team member, clambering up mountains with Terry Abraham.

And make no mistake about it; Terry *is* a Lakes Poet – just working with light and cloud and grass and water rather than stanzas and couplets.

The great Millom poet Norman Nicholson said that on a foul dark winter's night in West Cumbria he would think of his beloved tarn – lonely Devoke Water – and wonder 'what must it be like up there tonight'. Sometimes, when I know from his Twitter feed that Terry is wild camping in his little one-man tent in a blizzard, I think 'what must it be like for him up there tonight?', as I smugly reach from my couch for the thin mints and single malt.

In these pages you will read of an ascent we made of Sharp Edge while making *Blencathra*. During that hair-raising climb Terry turned to me as we clung for dear life to a bit of crag above a dizzying drop and said: "I won't be doing any drone footage today. I don't want to risk the equipment." Clearly I was part of the equipment that was more expendable. We made it, though, and it's in this book, along with much else about the landscape he loves and has made his own.

PART ONE

BEFORE SCAFELL PIKE

ONE OF THE THINGS MY GRANDMOTHER TOLD ME OFTEN WHEN I WAS A KID HAS STUCK WITH ME ALL MY LIFE: "MAKE THE MOST OF YOUR LIFE, TERRY..."

Becoming Abraham

My younger sister Anouska and I were brought up on a council estate, a nice enough mix of privately-owned and social housing in the Nottinghamshire village of Oxton by our mother Anna-Marie and, in the early years, our father, bus driver Terry Peel. A name was all we shared.

Things were never comfortable at home. My mum and my biological father, as I call him, fought frequently, and he was rarely around. I found out later he was having affairs, but I already knew he was abusive to my mother. I'd lie in bed at night as she screamed downstairs. When I tried to help her he'd beat me back. I remember being thrown down the stairs for standing up to her.

But that wasn't the only life I knew.

My mother's parents, Herbert and Lydia Abraham, lived on a farm in the village of Upton 15 miles away. I spent as much time on the farm as possible – including the whole of my six-week summer holiday – mucking in, playing, having fun. When the holidays ended I never wanted to go home.

I have a vivid memory from when I was six or seven years old. I'd been out all day, climbing trees, collecting conkers. When I returned home my grandparents were there with mother and the atmosphere was even worse than usual. I thought I was in trouble; I hadn't been climbing too high in the trees, I told them.

"Don't worry, you're not in trouble for that, Terry," they said. "Your dad's here."

I turned to see my biological father.

I was a confident, strong-minded lad by then. "Where've you been?," I asked. "We've not seen you for ages." I told him that instead of staying at the house I was off out.

When he insisted I stayed, things kicked off: "Who the hell are you? You're hardly ever here!"

At that, he went for me.

My grandfather stepped in: "You lay another finger on that boy and I'll shoot you," he told my father.

I believed him – he was a farmer, and I'd seen his guns.

So did my father. And it was soon after that, in the early 1980s, that my parents divorced.

Afterwards I adopted my grandfather's surname – my mother's maiden name – Abraham. It wasn't popular with my teachers and Social Services, but they let me stick with it. From then on – aged just seven – I became known as 'Abraham'. I formally changed my name by deed poll the moment I turned 18.

My youngest brother and sister – the twins Alexander and Claudine – were born in 1983, but we only ever saw Terry Peel again at meetings with Social Services.

◄
Pikes Crag and Scafell.

Culture shock

Our parents' divorce meant selling the family house. My mother, siblings and I moved to Hawtonville in Newark, and the transition from rural village to town life was a culture shock. In the countryside I'd been accustomed to seeing people only occasionally, but now folk were knocking on the door every five minutes. I used to escape by going out to play. I'd draw elaborate pictures on pavements with chalk and pastels, or sit in a corner somewhere with an art book or sketch pad. Sometimes I'd spend whole days out, creating black-and-white drawings and watercolours of the architecture around Newark. Mum never worried about me getting back late.

In the wake of the divorce my mother worked late shifts in pubs and as a waitress to pay the bills. She hadn't worked much before that – not in my lifetime at least – but now she worked to the point of exhaustion. While she lay in bed I'd look after my younger brother and sister, changing nappies in the night and, when they were older, taking them to school and feeding them while Mum either worked, slept, or – increasingly – cried. When the bailiffs came calling she hid behind the sofa.

We stayed in Hawtonville for two years before moving on again, this time to another council estate in Balderton on the southeast of Newark. It was here that I spent most of my childhood.

Mum understood what the divorce and house moves were putting me through. Later my grandmother showed me letters Mum had written to her. She wrote how she couldn't have coped without me looking after the kids. She described me as a "special young boy – special in his heart". I now understand my early life wasn't normal for most seven-year-olds. I suspect some of my junior school teachers were aware Mum was struggling after the divorce and tried to look out for me.

Even so, it was obvious I was different to the other kids at school. Unlike them, when I got home I had to be a man. I'd grown up too fast and ended up with an old man's head on a young man's shoulders when all I wanted was to go outside and play.

It was only on my grandparents' farm that I could be a child again.

> I'd grown up too fast and ended up with an old man's head on a young man's shoulders. It was only on my grandparents' farm that I could be a child again.

▸ A December dawn over the Scafells from Bowfell.

From Russia with love

My grandmother was born in Russia, growing up in the part of the country that was invaded by the Germans during the Second World War. She was incarcerated in a German concentration camp but survived because of her passion for English literature: she was able to read and speak English, so the Germans used her to translate intercepted Allied communications.

At the end of the war the German guards fled, leaving prisoners to fate. American forces arrived soon after. Grandmother wasn't a fan – she found them loud, brash and arrogant – but they gave the liberated prisoners a choice either to remain in Russia or to travel with them to new lives in Australia, America, Canada or Britain. Figuring that many members of her family would now be dead, Grandmother chose to emigrate and, because of her love of English literature, Britain became her new home. She trained as a nurse in Inverness and, once qualified, moved south to Lincoln.

My grandfather also survived the war. A German, he and the friends he'd grown up with served together as members of a U-boat crew. Few were to see the war's end. After months at sea, they put into a Spanish port for leave and despite being ordered not to fraternise with the locals, he and his crewmates went out on the town, got drunk and chatted up the local girls. He was spotted on the streets after curfew and shot by the notoriously strict German military police. He dodged the bullet – in fact it lodged in his skull; he still had the lump as an old man – and he was thrown into a cell, then transferred to military hospital. While he was recovering, his vessel returned to sea and was never seen again. That's Grandfather Abraham: one of the only servicemen who saw out the war because he was shot for fraternising with a Spanish lass.

By the time he was fit enough to return to service the tide was turning in the war and he had no wish to go back. His new U-boat crewmates felt the same. So once at sea they mutinied, ditching their captain in the ocean before heading towards Britain to surrender in the English Channel. Grandfather had survived the Battle of the Atlantic, but he arrived here as a prisoner of war and was placed in a PoW camp near Retford in Nottinghamshire, not far from Lincoln.

When the PoW camps closed, Grandfather became a gamekeeper, working for a landowner whose estate included a chunk of Sherwood Forest. When the landowner passed away he bequeathed an area of Brail Wood on the Sherwood Forest outskirts – something like 400 acres – to my grandfather. It enabled him to set up as a turkey farmer.

When I was a kid, Grandfather used to take me to a place he called 'Pets' Corner', near Retford. I didn't know why at the time, but it was very close to where he'd been held prisoner and I reckon he used to visit the site during those trips. The place and the people he was imprisoned with must have held special memories.

The rise of right-wing extremism frightens me because of what my grandparents went through. My grandmother used to drill the lessons of history into me and insist that I learn from the past. If you forget where you come from – if you forget your history – she would say, then the same mistakes will happen again and again. She believed human beings have a habit of repeating their mistakes every couple of generations because memories that are no longer fresh are forgotten.

> Our world was the outdoors: we'd wander the woods together and head off the beaten track to see wildlife, watch foxes and make dens. I still don't like sticking to paths.

▲ Wild camp on Stonesty Pike.

The path less travelled

Grandfather loved Britain's countryside and wildlife, and I went everywhere with him. Our world was the outdoors: we'd wander the woods together and head off the beaten track to see wildlife, watch foxes and make dens. I still don't like sticking to paths.

On one occasion he woke me at three in the morning and said: "Come on, we're going out." I loved it – until a moment when we were walking along a narrow track in the woods, I was chattering away and suddenly looked around to find him gone. I started wailing: "Grandad, Grandad, where are you?" Without warning, he jumped out of the bushes and scared the life out of me. He'd buggered off and hid, to test me.

▶ Sunset on Rampsgill Head.

◀ **Terry atop the great Whin Sill canyon of High Cup.**

I sat alone, captivated by the views, crepuscular light breaking through heavy cloud and shining on distant Windermere.

My grandmother's influence was academic. She dragged me around the country to museums, galleries and libraries. On rainy days I'd sit in her attic reading medical books and encyclopaedias she'd accrued over years of study. They fascinated me, to the extent that, when I was out on shoots with my grandfather I'd want to take animals apart to see how they worked.

As I ploughed my way through Grandmother's library of books I cultivated an interest in, and empathy with, people, history, heritage, nature and – most of all – the outdoors.

One of the things Grandmother told me often when I was a kid has stuck with me all my life: "Do you remember how things were before you were born? No? That's what it's like when you're dead. Make the most of your life, Terry."

First trip to Lakeland

For most of my childhood we never took family holidays, for the simple reason that we couldn't afford them. When I was really young there were a few breaks to a static caravan in Great Yarmouth, but they went out of the window when my siblings arrived and my parents divorced. After that, holidays were spent on my grandparents' farm instead.

That changed at the age of 13, when a school friend, Matthew Nicolson, and his family invited me to join them on their summer holiday in the Lake District.

It was the first time I had ever visited the National Park and I remember being blown away by it from day one. The moment I saw the fells I wanted to be on them, and when we arrived in Patterdale I told Matthew I was going straight up the nearest hill. From the summit of Place Fell I looked down, and, spying Matthew on the bridleway at Boredale Hause, I shouted for him to come up and join me. Together we stared at the view for what seemed like forever, before tearing back through the bracken.

His family spent the holiday in Patterdale Hotel while Matthew and I were dumped in the youth hostel. That was my first experience of a YHA hostel and I didn't much like it: it was all chores and sharing dorms with snoring men.

The days were different, though. Each morning an outdoors instructor from Patterdale Hall would take the two of us, along with a bunch of other kids, on walking, abseiling and orienteering adventures – at the end of one day I even got away with a cheeky pint in the White Lion.

One of the group walks turned into a watershed moment. The weather was miserable as we headed up Deepdale and on to Fairfield. We had our lunch on the summit and I sat alone, away from everyone else, captivated by the views, crepuscular light – I call the wandering beams 'God rays' – breaking through heavy cloud and shining on distant Windermere. As the rain worsened we made our way towards St Sunday Crag, where there was an almighty roar like a jet. Suddenly we were hit by a gust of wind with strength enough to pick people up and throw them through the air like dummies. I had no time to think before I was plucked off my feet, arms and legs flailing, and thrown to the ground head-first. Terrified of being blown off the fell, I crawled along on my hands and knees, desperate to get back to Patterdale.

I've only encountered such strong winds on two occasions since.

▶
Terry prepares to shoot on Little Mell Fell.
© Nathan Buckley.

◀
Sharp Edge on Blencathra.

All the world's problems could be solved, I thought, if people could be brought to places like this; these landscapes were capable of changing lives.

Those few minutes on the summit of Fairfield had, however, made a lasting impression on me.

All the world's problems could be solved, I thought, if people could be brought to places like this and given the chance to reflect on what was important in life; these landscapes were capable of changing lives. "I'm going to live here one day," I said to myself. "I want to spend the rest of my life among these fells."

It would be many years before I returned.

School, and James Bond

I felt out of place from the day I started secondary education at The Grove School in Newark. I came from a working-class background and lived on a council estate, while many of my classmates were from well-to-do homes with wealthy parents – a world that was alien to me. There was snobbery there too. I'd be mocked for being a working-class lad off the estate and some kids had a chip on their shoulder about me. I became particular about who I hung around with and in time I established a foot in both camps: during lunch breaks I'd hang out with mates from the estate, at other times I'd talk with the boffins – the 'boffs' from cleverer classes.

I excelled at athletics and long-distance running, particularly cross-country, which I much preferred to running in circles round a track. Then, as now, I enjoyed being battered by the elements and some of the coaches assumed – wrongly – that I was descended from Harold Abrahams, gold medal winner at the 1924 Paris Olympics in the 100-metre dash. Long-distance running demands more than just physical input: there's a lot of mind over matter, breaking things down into goals to enable you to keep going – to push your body to its limits.

I remember races in which I'd finish in the first ten, or even the top three, coughing up blood because of how hard I'd run. Any athlete will tell you that's not uncommon.

Thanks largely to my grandmother's influence, I also did well academically, coming either near or top of the class across a range of subjects. But my strengths lay in the arts – drawing and painting – and engineering. My teachers assumed I would go on to be an engineer or architect.

I formed a close bond with two teachers in particular: Paul Collingwood – who still lives in Newark; I'll see him for a pint in the pub when I go back – and my art teacher Moria Semple. She was keen on me focussing on art, while he would encourage me to widen my knowledge of technical subjects. But my passions didn't lay in either. Instead I nurtured a secret ambition: I dreamed of being a film maker, and very specifically, of producing *James Bond* movies.

My first films didn't amount to much. The school lent me a camcorder, but I was scared of damaging it, and the films were forgettable: the high point was a *Dracula*-style film for which I roped in mates and had them wander round a cemetery. Nor did I enjoy the process much. I had to edit in the camcorder because the school lacked an editing suite, and before long I jacked it in.

Nevertheless, I did well in my GCSEs. I took 12, as opposed to the usual eight or nine, and got Bs and Cs.

Expectations were high, therefore, when I started A-Levels. By then I was considered talented at art – technical drawing in particular – and loved drawing buildings. With my grandparents support, I was also encouraged to join evening courses.

For the first time in years I could see a future path: further education with a few *Dracula*-inspired films thrown into the mix.

Then my grandparents died.

Within a year of each other.

Losing my way

Grandmother died first, of a heart attack.

I was devastated. She'd been a second mother to me: I talked to her about things and learned stuff that I couldn't from Mum, who was always too stressed or busy with my siblings.

A year or so later we sensed something wasn't right with my grandfather – he hadn't been the man he had been since Grandmother died. I found his body on a visit to his home; a heart attack had killed him instantly.

My grandparents' deaths cast a deep and lasting shadow on the years to come. While I'd felt like a father figure to my siblings, Grandfather had been a father to me, fulfilling a role that my biological father had been unable to. Gone was the escapism – and chance to be a kid again – that had been offered on the farm.

I dropped two A-levels and ended up taking just art with art history and drama. Instead of studying, I had run-ins with teachers who were disappointed that I was off doing my own thing instead of turning up to lessons. I got into fights with other students and instead of socialising in the common room would be off in a music room playing piano alone. I bunked off lessons and started hitting the pubs.

With the benefit of hindsight I realise I was in a depression. You can see it in a lot of my drawings from the time – scenes filled with gothic monsters and deformed figures.

I flunked my A-levels.

Then I quit education for good.

I'd applied to university to study art and

▲
Cairn Toul, Cairngoms National Park.

Instead of socialising in the common room I'd be off in a music room playing piano alone. I bunked off lessons and started hitting the pubs.

animation because of my interest in film and because I thought that if I was going to get in anywhere it would be on the strength of my art. And even though my results – C in art and a D in drama – were good enough for me to be offered a couple of places I didn't take the applications further. I was done with academia.

The pubs beckon

After completing my A-levels, I started earning a few quid working part-time behind the bar at the Fox and Crown in Appleton Gate, Newark. That's when I developed my love for real ales. I'd drink Castle Rock Brewery's Hemlock Bitter, and Springhead Brewery's Roaring Meg IPA – both good beers. It was the era of the alcopop, but I wasn't interested – I was an old fart even then.

I found a way to make a little extra cash at the Fox and Crown by drawing portraits of customers' pets – and sometimes of the customers themselves. Before long I was making good money from it. The pub owner displayed my pictures in the bar. People would see them and ask me to do work for them. At one point I even did artist's impressions for architects. I specialised in black-and-white pencil drawings, though I also loved painting, which allowed me to be more expressive: it was about emotion and trying to convey it on canvas, whether the subject was a landscape, person or building. The real money, though, was in black-and-white pencil drawings of customers' horses, dogs and cats. As the money built up I wondered whether I really was missing out by not going to uni. I was probably already doing what I'd do with a degree anyway.

Even as the animal commissions piled up, I'd not lost my passion for film. So juggling shifts at the Fox and Crown, I started on a BTEC course in media studies at Newark College. I lasted nine months before quitting; there wasn't enough practical learning – I wanted to grab a camera, get out and shoot. There's only so much you can learn about film making and photography in the classroom. The rest of it is about getting into the field and pressing 'record'.

The pet portraits were at the point of turning into a potential career. Through the pub, a few local businessmen helped me draw up a plan to rent a shop in town where I could display drawings and paintings, and where people could come in to commission work.

Having come from a comparatively poor background I found myself earning good money – and bloody hell did I know how to spend it!

▲ **Recognition from the brewing world: Sharp Edge bitter inspired by *Life of a Mountain: Blencathra.***

The bank liked the idea but didn't like the debts I'd accrued at college. They also wanted me to get more managerial business experience. The disappointment forced me to ask myself where I wanted to take my career.

I decided to work in pubs full time.

I was good at what I did, and my hands-on, practical approach enabled me to work my way up the ladder. I left the Fox and Crown when an opportunity arose at the Hobgoblin in Newark's Market Place. A year later, I crossed the road and started work at a Wetherspoon pub, The Sir John Arderne. And that was it: a new career door opened.

Within a year and a half I was a manager and shortly after that I became a trouble-shooter for the chain: I'd be sent to sort out failing Wetherspoon branches, managing both the business side of things and the troublemakers. I wasn't afraid to get my hands dirty and get into scraps – and the resulting revenue turnaround was usually good, for which I'd get bonuses.

Having come from a comparatively poor background I found myself earning good money – and bloody hell did I know how to spend it! Being able to buy decent clothes and take trips away was all new to me. On nights out with work colleagues I'd pay for drinks, cabs, club entry fees – the lot. When I look back now I'm mortified by how much money I pissed up the wall. But it was a rite of passage and probably a mechanism for coping with the stress of the job. It was also good fun.

After a few years, I all but forgot about drawing and painting. The career didn't leave time or energy for much else, including relationships. While I enjoyed the work – and the lifestyle it was buying me – I knew it couldn't last forever. I'd lost touch with the outdoors, with countryside and nature, the things I'd loved doing with Grandfather since I was a boy. And film? It felt like an impossible dream.

▲
Terry in his younger years: a mix of partying (left, in blue with friend Eion Cartledge) and wild camps (right).

▶
Summer dawn panorama from Esk Pike.

Settling down

I met Sue in January 2004. I was 27 and had been crashing at Mum's house back in Newark.

I'd left Wetherspoon a few years before – the violent side of work hadn't suited me – before moving from one job to another, gradually making my way back home north where I always found the people to be friendlier.

By now I had a bit of money stashed away, which I reckoned would sort me out for a while, and I was going through a bachelor phase: out every weekend – if not most nights – chasing girls and partying.

It was on one of these nights out that I met my wife-to-be.

Sue and I first met in a nightclub: I was trying to charm some of her friends on behalf of mates who were too chicken-shit. I wasn't so bashful. I'd go up: "Blah blah blah... Oh, by the way, my mate over there would like a chat." They weren't interested, so I went back and told my mate, but then one of the girls came over to say that one her friends was interested in me. She scrawled her phone number on a piece of card in lipstick alongside a name – 'Sue'.

When I searched for the card a few days later I couldn't find it – Mum must have inadvertently thrown it away. So when I bumped into Sue a couple of weeks later her mates grilled me about why I'd not got back to her. I told them I wasn't looking for anything serious.

Later that night my friends told me they were going back to the club as one of them was interested in one of Sue's friends. I was more interested in getting a Chinese takeaway and going home, but they persuaded me by offering to buy the drinks. There I saw Sue again, and found I really liked her.

Initially I was cautious. I'm a creature of habit and by now I was used to my bachelor ways. I liked her but realised I'd met someone who could rip my heart out, chuck it in a paper bag and set it on fire. Still, I thought I might hang around with her for a bit – see what happened.

Sue had grown up on a farm in Oxfordshire in the Chilterns. I appreciated the fact that she was a country girl who liked me for being me – she wasn't the sort to try to change me. I respected her privacy and her sense of independence, and I always say that our marriage works because we don't form a single circle. Instead we're two circles combined with a big overlapping area. We don't necessarily share all our interests.

A few months after that night in Time and Diva nightclub, Sue and I were driving around and saw some beat bandits racing in their cars. I said to Sue: "Think of all the money they've wasted on fuel to do that – they could have spent that going to the Lake District."

Sue said she'd never been. Never been to the Lakes!? "Christ," I said, "you'd love it."

Two weeks later – boom – we're off to the

Lakes. We bought cheap camping kit from Woolworths and headed away on a trip that neither of us will forget. Driving around Ullswater opposite Place Fell, we looked towards Glenridding and the scene towards Helvellyn brought everything back to me. It was heaven on earth, and Sue loved it too. We camped at the Brotherswater Inn campsite, which was a quiet site back then.

Sue still says that I tried to kill her that weekend. I took her on the same route I still vaguely remembered from when I'd first visited the Lakes as a kid. The plan was to head along Deepdale and walk up to Deepdale Hause between Fairfield and St Sunday Crag, then head over St Sunday Crag and back to Patterdale where we were parked. Like an idiot, I was using a print-off 1:50,000-scale Ordnance Survey map, and we took a wrong turning which resulted in us scrambling among crags on Fairfield. Sue was frightened to death and I was shaking. It was only as we approached the summit of St Sunday Crag that I realised we should have taken a completely different route.

She didn't talk to me all the way to the top.

My nerves finally caught up with me on the steep path down to Patterdale. It's airy in places, but somehow all the fear in Sue had evaporated and she was skipping down like a kid, scaring the hell out of me, a big smile on her face.

That trip reignited my passion for the outdoors. After that, every spare weekend we would go to the Lakes, the Peak District or Snowdonia.

I can vividly remember, when I was in my early 20s, saying to my mates they would all be married with kids before me – that I would be in my early 30s before getting married. And that's exactly what happened.

Four years after our first adventure in the Lakes, Sue forced my hand. One rainy day we were in Wimpy in Newark when she started asking where our relationship was heading. She persisted until eventually I had to say: "I was actually going to propose to you this New Year's Eve!"

> Scrambling among the crags on Fairfield, Sue was frightened to death and I was shaking. She didn't talk to me all the way to the top.

I'd had it arranged for a while: a plan to surprise her by proposing at a hotel in the Lakes. Her face lit up. She was thrilled. "Oh! Pretend I never heard that!" she said, but the moment we left Wimpy we were shopping for a ring.

We spent much of that New Year's Eve in the lounge at the Fish Inn in Buttermere. The weather was horrible but we were happy in each other's company, relaxed and reading. Eventually I looked at the clock, realised it was midnight – 2007 had arrived – and I asked her to be my wife.

The proposal, she told me, didn't count; I was too tipsy on port. I swear on my life I wasn't – I'd been waiting for midnight so that I could have a beer after popping the question – but no, she insisted I do it again the following day.

I asked her to choose a romantic spot and next morning we drove to Surprise View in Borrowdale.

"Here'll do," she said, as we pulled up.

"OK. Inside the car or outside?"

"Outside. I'll sit on that bench and you can get down on one knee."

▲
Evening sun from a camp on Crinkle Crags.

◄
Room with a view: overnight stay in Great Langdale.

It was then that I noticed a police car parked nearby.

"So?" asked Sue.

"It's a personal thing, but I don't want to get down on one knee in front of the police. What the hell are they doing here anyway?"

It turned out they were part of security arrangements for a member of the royal family visiting the area. So I got down on one knee and proposed – and the officers got out of their car and started clapping. It wasn't the reaction I'd anticipated, but I didn't much mind – my second proposal, Sue confirmed, counted. It had taken her four years to get me to do something respectable, she told me.

We were married the following year, on 26 May, 2008. I was 32.

Heart attack

Sue saved me, in a way. We'd met at a period in my life when I was at a loose end, in and out of various jobs, and she provided the support and faith I needed to become settled, find stable employment and start earning decent money again.

Just before we met I had started working as a chef at Pizza Express. I was with them for three years over the period when we became engaged and got married.

That was also the time when I had my suspected heart attack.

I was about 29 when I started experiencing heart murmurs and palpitations. I would feel my heart flutter and bump, and sometimes skip a beat. I'd think: "Whoa, what happened there?" Plenty of people get it – it's normal, I'd tell myself – but I was experiencing palpitations frequently, sometimes daily, and they worsened over a six-month period.

Although increasingly anxious, I kept my health concerns to myself. I was stressed by the pressure of the job, I reasoned; the flutters would pass. Besides, I was pretty fit; I worked out with weights – though I wondered if my workouts might also be affecting me.

I got down on one knee and proposed – and the police officers got out of their car and started clapping. It wasn't the reaction I'd anticipated.

One night, at around one in the morning, I awoke suddenly, feeling as though someone was standing on my chest. I sat up, unable to breathe, and woke Sue. I spilled the beans and confessed things hadn't been right for a while. This, though, was a whole new level of pain.

Sue made me dial 999 and they wanted to send an ambulance immediately. But I didn't want to cause hassle. So Sue drove me to A&E at half-one in the morning, and, by the time they'd wired me up to an ECG monitor I was

▲ **Scafell Pike and buttresses.**

▶ **Langdale Pikes inversion.**

feeling fine again, laughing and joking with the nurses. Then the doctor came back in with the paperwork and I just knew, seeing his face, that something was wrong. He sat down to chat with me and described the workings of the heart. He showed me some graphs – a bit like the screens you see on TV hospital dramas – with the bump line; one, two, three. Where there should have been a fourth bump, the graph was practically flat. The doctor couldn't tell me what it was, or what was causing it.

The doctor's words hit me hard. I started thinking about all the things I still wanted to do, all the places I wanted to see – Scotland, and, of course, the Lake District.

Over the next year I was in and out of hospital as doctors carried out more tests. For a while I had to wear a portable ECG with a data recorder, 24 hours a day.

One day, while working in my garage, I stepped out for a cigarette and started to cry. I couldn't believe this was happening. I thought of Sue and my step-kids, Fiona and Josh, of the bills and money. "Please don't kill me off now; there's so much I want to give the world," I said, to no-one in particular.

At the end of that period I had another appointment with a heart specialist. He was accompanied by two young nurses and asked if I minded them being present while he carried out some tests. He had me blowing into machines, walking on a treadmill. I'll never forget what he said to the nurses as he conducted an ultrasound test on my heart: "You can tell that this is a young man, very fit and active, by how developed and strong his heart is. It's the heart of an ox." After all that, he told me that he could find nothing wrong with my heart. And I never heard from them again.

The health scare made me rethink my lifestyle. I became determined to spend more time in the outdoors, in the landscapes I loved and from which work had distracted me for a large chunk of my adult life.

I thought of Sue and the step-kids, of the bills and money. "Please don't kill me off now; there's so much I want to give the world," I said, to no-one in particular.

On my very first visit to the Lakes I had wondered idly what it might be like to spend nights out on the tops rather than down in the valley-bottom guest houses and B&Bs. But it was many years later that I first typed 'wild camping' into Google. I was stunned to learn such an activity existed – that you could take a tent and camp out on the tops. It was exactly what I wanted to do.

Wild camping, or backpacking, wasn't widely recognised at the time. There was the Backpackers Club and *The Great Outdoors* magazine, neither of which I had heard of until I started my research. As I started to read the magazine and the gear features by a chap called Chris Townsend, I realised that I needed to get hold of some decent kit so that I didn't have to carry an impossibly heavy load, like kids on Duke of Edinburgh award expeditions onto the tops.

▲
Terry directing shepherdess Alison O'Neill (top), and a break during the filming of *Helvellyn* (below).

◄
Unnamed tarn on Hard Knott overlooking the Scafells.

One of my first wild camps was in the Lake District in the depths of winter with old friend Eion Cartledge. Neither of us drove, so we travelled by public transport and walked into Seathwaite from Keswick with the aim of camping out on Scafell Pike. We were so exhausted when we got there that the family at Seathwaite Farm let us kip in one of their outbuildings. These days it's a bunkhouse but back then it was just a barn. They told us that another guy was already staying there, a professional photographer, and we found him still awake when we got back from a meal in the pub. As we chatted with him by the light of our head torches I couldn't understand why he kept looking at the floor rather than me. I wondered if he had some kind of nervous twitch, but didn't want to embarrass him by asking, so I said nothing. It was only the next day that Eion informed me that my thermals had ripped between my legs, and my cock and balls had been hanging out – that was why the photographer had been looking everywhere but at me.

We did get to camp on Scafell Pike – but we did so in a snowstorm. Eion snored while the storm raged outside, wind pushing the roof of the tent flush with my face as the night hours slowly passed. "What are we doing here?," I asked myself at some godforsaken hour of the morning. But I loved it – absolutely loved it. And I wanted more.

We had a hell of a time wading off the fell next day through the snow – I'm afraid to say that we didn't have crampons, though we did at least have spikes on our boots – and the Langdale valley had been snowed in with drifts to the top of walls. Cars couldn't get in or out, so we ploughed on and on to Ambleside where the snow was thinner and we could catch a bus north. In Keswick we were amazed to find there had been no snow at all – that it was another world down in the Langdales.

▲ **Terry on one of his favourite fells; Ingleborough.**

"What are we doing here?" I asked myself at some godforsaken hour of the morning. But I loved it – absolutely loved it. And I wanted more.

Looking back now, I'm mortified that we even went out; neither of us had ever experienced winter conditions before.

But I have very fond memories of that trip. It was another little character-building baptism of fire, and I always thrive on a challenge.

Vlogs and redundancy

Blogs are two-a-penny these days. Back in 2010, however, when I set up terrybnd.blogspot.com to share my early adventures in wild camping online, outdoor blogs were few and far between. Partly for that reason, it quickly built a loyal audience of followers.

▲
Esk Pike rising above an inversion while filming *Scafell Pike*.

At the time I was working for a computer security service in Newark and spending weekends on the moors and mountains, wild camping at every opportunity. To accompany the blog I used a cheap digital camcorder and recorded footage at camp. In doing so I reignited my passion for film.

It was a defining time: out there on the fells I was combining for the first time the two things I loved most – the outdoors and film – and I realised that was what I wanted to do with the rest of my life.

I began developing my craft, teaching myself the basics of film making – you need an establishing shot, close-ups, low angles for things that look threatening, different angles for scenes that are intimidating. I was slowly learning the language of film and its unique vocabulary.

During that period I made a video of the Peak District which, if viewed now, feels like a mini *Life of a Mountain* film. It's about five minutes long and lacks any talking, but it caught the attention of a gentleman who had a business promoting Peak District holiday cottages. He asked if he might buy the film to help promote the area. He subsequently offered me more work. So it was that I found myself moonlighting – working with an anti-virus company in the week and making outdoors films at weekends.

That year we got a new boss at work. My impression was that he didn't like me – that he thought I exerted too much influence on the team. In December 2010 they told me I was to be made redundant. As part of the process I had to attend an interview with my bosses. Nominally, it was to discuss ways I might be able to stay with the company, but in reality it was a formal obligation. The writing was on the wall for my career. I kept everything in the interview constructive. I argued with evidence and facts. But my new boss didn't want me in the business; he wanted me out. Within half an hour my career was over. Half an hour after that I went home and bawled my eyes out.

▲ **Stormy sunset: the Eastern Fells from Terry's home.**

◀ **The Jaws of Borrowdale from Latrigg.**

Out there on the fells I was combining for the first time the two things I loved most – the outdoors and film – and I realised that was what I wanted to do with the rest of my life.

Big break

The redundancy papers arrived in January 2011.

It was a bad time for me. I felt angry and humiliated, but several friends said: "Terry, this could be the best thing that has ever happened to you." They encouraged me to refocus – to look at producing my outdoor videos full-time.

I considered it. The computer security outfit had given me a reasonable redundancy package – three months' worth of pay – so I invested in a camera to make a go of it. It would have been easy enough to return to pub work, but I wanted to demonstrate that I could bounce back after the redundancy by following a passion. Besides, the draw of the fells was stronger than ever.

I was continuing to learn film making on the hoof, honing my craft and selling the occasional promotional video. For the next year we lived off Sue's income and on what little I could earn. One month I might bring in £200, the next a few more hundred quid, but it still wasn't enough to cover all the bills, especially as Fiona and Josh were still at home. We leaned heavily on credit cards. Eventually, Sue said: "We can't do this any more. You need to bring more money in."

That was when I got my big break.

In early 2012, Staffordshire County Council invited me to a meeting in their Stafford offices. Staffordshire's patch of the Peak District National Park was often overlooked by visitors in favour of Derbyshire's, so the council's tourism department commissioned me to make a video promoting their area, including the Roaches, the Upper Dove Valley, and towns and villages such as Leek and Longnor. Attractions like Alton Towers, the Caldon Canal and the Churnet Valley Railway were included, as were outdoor activities such as parascending, climbing, mountain biking and walking.

It was good money, but there was a tight deadline – and I couldn't afford to mess up.

A lot of the landscape featured was new ground for me, but I turned round the six-minute video – which included some basic aerial footage – on deadline. The launch in a fancy hotel attracted people from various businesses and tourism organisations. The lights went out, the video played, and when the six minutes ended there was silence. "They hate it," I thought, and walked to the bar. The next thing I knew everyone was piling out to congratulate me, handing me business cards and going nuts for it. I look back at the film now and reckon it's cheesy, but at the time their response was the confidence boost I needed.

A few weeks later I had another break – a call from Rob Birrell, marketing director at AMG, parent company of outdoor equipment brand Vango – inviting me to a meeting in Glasgow. I thought, "Hold on, that's a lot of money travelling to Glasgow from Newark. What's this all about?"

It turned out they'd seen a video on my blog which included a Vango tent. I thought perhaps Vango wanted to offer me a tent in return, but it was more than that; they wanted me to accompany them on a photoshoot to take pictures for their catalogue.

It was a modest gig at first, but not long after that I went with them to a bigger shoot in the Alps, which was a first for me. I've worked with other companies since, but I've stuck with Vango, partly out of loyalty and mainly because I have a good relationship with them, particularly with Rob.

By the end of that first year of freelancing things had improved financially. But I still wasn't where I wanted to be. Sure, I was making films, but since the age of 13 my heart had belonged to the Lake District, and I desperately wanted to get back. What I had in mind for my next career step was a grand project: a documentary that would be called *Life of a Mountain: Scafell Pike.*

Since I was 13 years old my heart had belonged to the Lake District, and I desperately wanted to get back. What I had in mind for my next career step was a grand project: a documentary that would be called *Life of a Mountain: Scafell Pike.*

▲
Terry enjoying a break from filming. © Nathan Buckley.

PART TWO

SCAFELL PIKE

I'D CAPTURE SCAFELL PIKE ON COUNTLESS CAMPS AND THE FINISHED FILM WOULD SHOWCASE THE FELL THROUGH EACH OF THE SEASONS. THERE WOULD BE NO NARRATOR: THE MOUNTAIN WOULD SPEAK FOR ITSELF.

This one goes out to the one I love

Life had turned around. A year earlier I'd been shown the door from work, and my self-confidence had taken a beating. Now I was rediscovering my twin loves of the outdoors and film making, and was building a new career from scratch, wild camping at every opportunity. Best of all, I was being paid to immerse myself in those passions.

Even so, my creative side was frustrated by the constraints of corporate videos and the restrictions of fulfilling the demands of others. My dream had never been a career making short commercial videos; I had a different itch that needed scratching.

Instead I wanted to make a *film* – a documentary. In fact, I envisaged a series of three, each focussed on one of the national three peaks: England's Scafell Pike, Ben Nevis in Scotland and Snowdon in Wales. At the same time I wanted to get back to Cumbria and the Lake District, which I had come to regard as my spiritual home: cut me and I bleed Lakeland. For entirely selfish reasons, therefore, I decided instead to base my trilogy in Lakeland.

Of all the corners of the National Park, the one I love most is Wasdale. That love inspired what was to be my first documentary – a cinematic diary of a year in the life of Scafell Pike. I'd capture Scafell Pike on countless camps and the finished film would showcase the fell through each of the seasons. There would be no narrator: the mountain would speak for itself, through its scenery and through the voices of the people who lived in the shadow of the fell, who worked on it and who cared for it.

Next, I thought, would come Helvellyn, a personal favourite and my kind of fell, similar in scenery and drama to the Scafells. The series would close with Blencathra and Skiddaw, two fells that are joined at the hip: when people talk about the Back o' Skiddaw, they're talking about the hinterland of both Skiddaw and Blencathra – the Forest to the north of the fells is one glorious prairied mass.

I had no preconceptions about, or even expectations of, a target audience. *Scafell Pike* would be a personal film – one that reflected what I found interesting in the area. I wanted to cast the net wide to craft a true portrait, and my hope was that if I could get people to watch it they might be inspired.

Nor would the film just be landscapes and natural drama: there would also be an educational element, so that Lakes-lovers and walkers like myself could learn a little, as might someone who's never set foot in the high places before. I wanted to put the film together in such a way that it would inspire, educate, enlighten and reveal something of the mountain's spiritual nature.

◄
Winter sunrise from the summit memorial cairn, Scafell Pike.

Spiritual, yes, and never rushed. Not that anything is *ever* rushed around Wasdale; the rat race bypasses that Lakeland backwater. Some might find life in the valley slow – though in the years since I started shooting, that approach has become fashionable; I was making 'slow TV' long before it hit the media headlines.

The vision for my planned film was part driven by the frustration I felt watching big-budget TV documentaries. I've never understood why travel programme makers so often head off to far-flung countries when there's a wealth of beauty on our doorstep. Even programmes about the Lakes never show what I experience when I'm wild camping. The production teams are never there to film, say, a temperature inversion, or capture the richness of colours at sunset or sunrise.

There's plenty of reasons for that. Professional film units run on fixed schedules – crews are typically hired on hourly rates – and they might not have the slightest interest in the subject of the documentary they are working on. To many it's just another job, and few are inclined to go the extra mile. They also have health and safety to bear in mind, along with the associated red tape. As an independent film maker committed to my own projects I have no such constraints; I can do what the hell I like.

A journey, however, starts with the first step. And while the idea of a trilogy appealed, it lay a long way off. First there was Scafell Pike: a formidable mountain in a remote valley, which I was attempting to film using a one-man crew. Things were not going to be easy.

Strapped for cash

The first challenge I faced was financial.

I needed cash to get my dream off the ground. And I needed to be realistic: a budget would have to cover not only production costs, but also a fee to enable me to pay bills, keep up mortgage payments and feed the family while filming and editing.

Some might find life in Wasdale slow – though in the years since I started shooting, that approach has become fashionable.

I made informal approaches to potential sponsors, including gear manufacturers Rab and Vango, to test the waters. I told them I had an idea for a film – one that was likely to take at least a year, possibly 18 months to produce (in fact it would take more than two years). In return for any support they could have their logos in the title sequence. If they showed any interest, I said, I would put together a formal proposal on paper.

Both came back almost immediately: they loved the idea. No need for anything formal, they said, just ping over an invoice. They essentially said, "How much do you want?" and left me to it.

I was taken aback. Their response was a vote of confidence – not only in the project, but also in me. Their unconditional support also meant I could drop everything and head off to Wasdale to focus on the first *Life of a Mountain* film, and I'll always be grateful to Rob Birrell at AMG and Nikki Skinner at Rab who invested such faith in me at the outset.

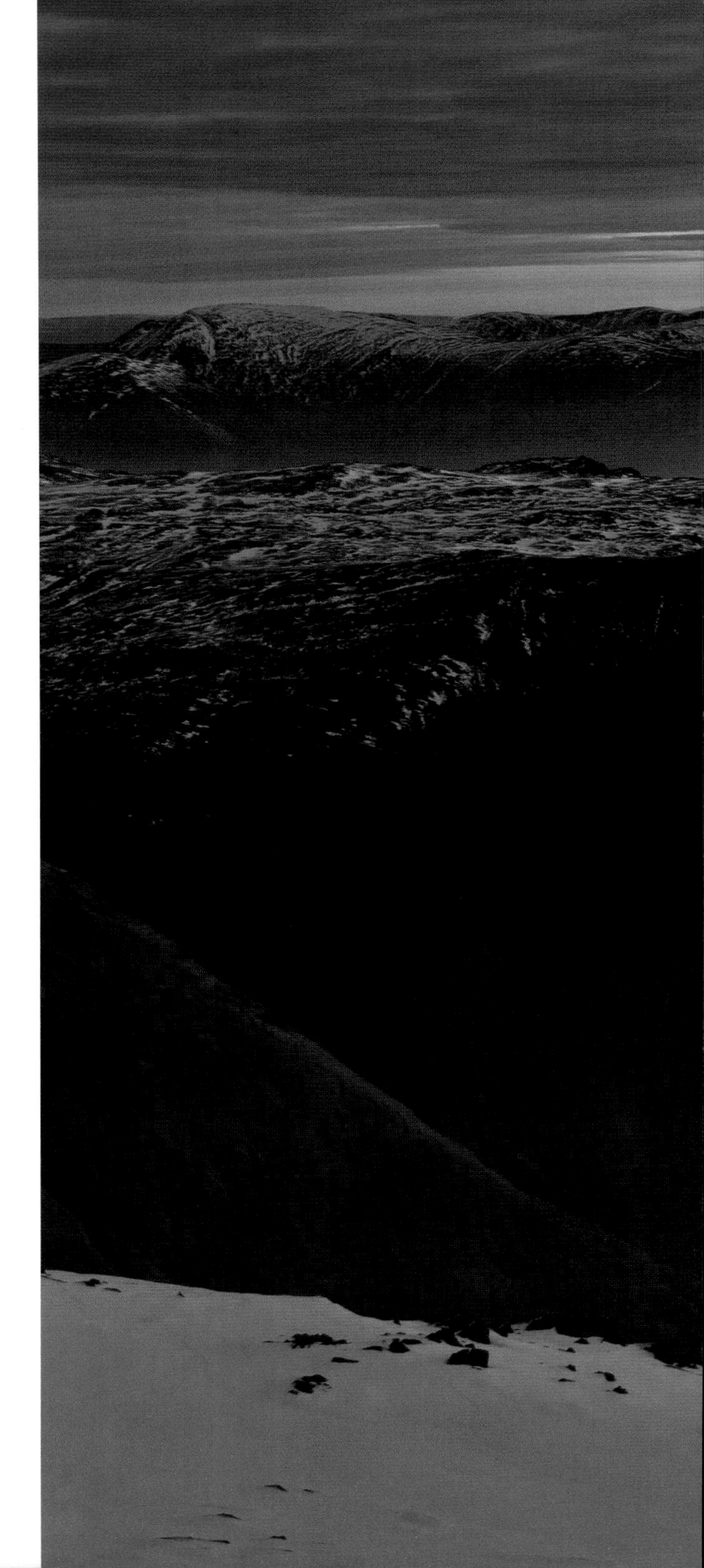

▶ **Drama and light on the Langdale Pikes.**

▲
Countess Bridge and the head of Wasdale.

Home from home

If I've ever had a second home, then it has been The Strands Inn, Nether Wasdale. It is one of those locals you have to seek out, set among the woods and low-lying hills of Wasdale. The view from The Strands – of white-washed cottages overtopped by the distant screes – is sublime.

Mark and Lesley Corr, who own the pub and its microbrewery, were a massive help to me when making *Life of a Mountain: Scafell Pike*. If the weather was poor they'd give me a spare room for the night so I didn't have to camp in the beer garden or a farmer's field. They provided me with food and drink – they even brought breakfast over to my tent some mornings. I filmed a scene in the pub with photographer Mark Gilligan as a thank you to them.

As with the folks at the Wasdale Head Inn, Mark and Lesley accepted my food deliveries from Asda and gave me provisions to take back onto the fells. They let me recharge my equipment or leave kit with them when it wasn't needed for a shoot. When filming finally ended they even wrote off my bar tab.

Although I don't get over there much these days, I still love returning to Wasdale. It's so different to the rest of the Lake District, with life moving at a different pace. As the valley head comes into view all the memories flood back – I remember trekking the lonely lakeside road from Nether Wasdale to Wasdale Head, six miles in the rain carrying all my kit and food and God-knows-what. But walking into The Strands to catch up with the locals and my friends – and when Mark and Lesley give me a big hug – I feel like I've never been away.

Mark had set up a microbrewery at The Strands within a year of moving in, back in 2006. At the last count, Cumbria has more microbreweries than any other English county, and while some have come and gone, been bought out or expanded and rebranded, Mark

▲
Home from home: The Strands Inn, Nether Wasdale.

has kept his the way it's always been. After I finished the Scafell film, Mark produced a Scafell Summit beer and used one of my pictures on the label. It was one of the proudest moments of my life.

Sure, I had a film to my name.

But now I also had my own beer...

Sure, I had a film to my name. But now I also had my own beer...

Making plans

In the early days of production I didn't have much of an idea about how I'd structure the film. The story I wanted the film to tell would, I imagined, evolve gradually as filming progressed. Certain aspects would have to be thought out – I'd need specific opening and closing scenes, and I wanted to end the documentary on a visual high. Beyond that I was working blind.

In the end, *Life of a Mountain: Scafell Pike* was as much about people as the mountain, and looking back, I struck lucky with who I invited to appear in the film. I was fortunate, too, that those people were willing to take part. At the time few knew who I was or understood what I was hoping to achieve. When approaching people I was often met with suspicion and cynicism – and not everyone was willing to appear in front of the camera. Some changed their minds and became more forthcoming after seeing clips I put on my phone to show people in pubs.

The pubs played an important – if unlikely – role in the creative process. Because the Western Fells lie in such a remote rural area, pubs are the beating heart of the communities they serve. When visitors come to the Lakes they see a place that's busy with holidaymakers. But when the tourists have gone it quietens down, and the village halls, shepherds' meets and pubs are where locals head to catch up with friends and neighbours. It was largely in pubs that I found those I included in *Scafell Pike* – particularly the farmers.

Folk in the film: Mark Richards – and a love of the quiet life

Guidebook author Mark Richards is like a jolly, year-round Santa Claus. He loves to chat to people – to discover what inspires them to take to the fells, or what guidebook they're using. Before the Scafells film I'd known Mark through his guidebooks; his linescape work is similar to Alfred Wainwright's and I was aware he had an actual connection with Wainwright – Mark and his wife Helen knew him well, and AW encouraged Mark's talent for pen-and-ink drawing.

Mark's mind is constantly on the go – as well as engaging with everyone he meets, ideas constantly flow from his imagination, and

▲ Guidebook writer Mark Richards: 'A jolly, year-round Santa Claus'.

When the tourists have gone it quietens down, and the village halls, shepherds' meets and pubs are where locals head to catch up with friends and neighbours.

his enthusiasm for life is unquenchable. But sometimes – particularly when trying to film a scene – that endless energy can be frustrating. Thankfully, over the years we've become good enough friends for me to say to him: "Pack it in, Mark, and focus!" If I clock any members of the public approaching, I'll say; "Don't talk to them! If they say 'hello', say 'hello' back and leave it at that. Let's get this scene out of the way: once it's done, you can do what you want!"

Unlike Mark, when I'm on the fells I'm often antisocial; I'd rather be on my own. But when I'm working on people scenes one of the key skills I've had to develop is learning how to put them at ease. The best results come when they feel relaxed, which means having a laugh and some banter and allowing them to be themselves. I tell people to forget the camera is there and to talk directly to me. That can be awkward when I have to hand-hold the camera, but if I can perch it on a tripod and stand off-camera they become less self-conscious. Then I'll either edit the footage and show it to them, which boosts their confidence, or show them clips from other scenes to give them an idea of what I'm aiming for.

Over the years I've got better at shooting the people side of the films – though it doesn't always work; not everyone is confident enough to convey their story or express their feelings on film. That can make for tricky editing if I want to include a scene without switching off an audience – though on the flip side that uneasiness lends footage a layer of realism, and that element of organic authenticity is important to me.

Nothing is scripted: I might prompt subjects with questions or encourage them to emphasise a certain point, but it all comes across in their own voice. When blended in with everything else, those voices are part of the magic.

Folk in the film: Nutty Professor Iain and mountain camaraderie

'Nutty Professor Iain', I call him. Fix the Fells upland ranger Iain Gray is as lovely as they come. He's intelligent, thoughtful and extremely knowledgeable about the fells. Although naturally shy, that doesn't come across in *Scafell Pike*, to which he made a great contribution.

► A gloomy autumn day in Eskdale.

He is dedicated to mountain environments – when working he's on the fell; on holiday he walks in Scotland – and I think that comes across. Iain's never off the mountains and I'm convinced he'll never leave that job.

I wanted to include Fix the Fells rangers because the work they do repairing upland paths is such an important part of maintaining the fabric of the mountain environment. Fix the Fells is overseen by the National Trust, which was one of the film's sponsors, but there was no pressure to include them; the Trust was aware I wouldn't be dictated to – that I would only include what I wanted, and only if it was likely to work in the context of the film.

As I was setting up my tripod to film the Fix the Fells team working on repairs to the Scafell Pike path, I became aware of the banter between them. There was great chemistry, of the kind that only comes from working so tightly together over time. They've become mates – out together in all weathers and conditions – who've developed their own camaraderie, an ability to lift their mood and morale when fixing paths or clearing drains on a dreary day. I told them to forget I was there and just be themselves. I positioned myself a short distance away from them and, over time, they became less aware of me. Their relaxed mood enabled me to capture little moments of banter. It was very natural. The rangers are highly skilled, yet they're not well remunerated. They seem to draw their reward from job satisfaction and the tough environment in which they work.

The National Trust were fantastic in helping me out, offering free camping pods and other support. I had to approach them for permission to film on their land – which might seem odd to many people because Wasdale Head is a wild place, not a stately home – but they did not impose any conditions, other than an expectation that I would contact the local ranger to let them know whenever I would be camping out. I never did, though; with the way I work, it was hardly practical – I went out when I went out.

▲ **The Fix the Fells team work on the path into Brown Tongue.**

◄ **Wasdale reflections.**

> The Fix the Fells team draw their reward from job satisfaction and from the environment in which they work.

Above the cloud

At the time of the Scafell film, Carey Davies was hillwalking officer with the British Mountaineering Council (BMC). I wanted to include the BMC, to raise awareness of the organisation and the work it does for walkers and climbers, but I specifically wanted the BMC to be represented by Carey, a young lad who communicates well.

Carey is a passionate mountain man – though I don't agree with him on everything and occasionally enjoyed enlightening him on things like the historical campaign for a right of access to mountains. Like many people, he traced its roots back to the Kinder mass trespass of 1932, but the first protest was actually on Latrigg in the Lake District in August 1887. Two-thousand people marched to the summit of Latrigg and several were taken to court in Carlisle – including National Trust co-founder Canon Hardwicke Rawnsley. But history has largely overlooked this Cumberland trespass, perhaps because the press was based in Manchester and the capital back then.

Carey was easy to work with, and it was a good and easy day's shoot. I was camped on Esk Pike and had arranged to meet him around Esk Hause as he came up from Borrowdale. Knowing I'd be there before him, I headed down to Grains Gill, the top of the ghyll from Seathwaite, to meet him. Because the weather was bad higher up, I filmed him there, then suggested we head towards my camp as the weather improved. There had been an inversion earlier in the morning and when we got up there, the cloud had sunk again. It was beautiful to capture on camera and added much to the scene, which would otherwise have been set against grey mirk.

I blended the Carey sequence with material I'd already filmed with the Fix the Fells team. I think about correlations between scenes much more these days and, when capturing footage on the fells, shoot a lot of additional footage. A BBC cameraman who filmed me making *Scafell Pike* advised me to shoot everything – even if it didn't catch my eye. "You can never have enough rope," he said. "There might come a day when you're doing an edit and you realise you need a shot you rejected at the time. No matter how boring it is or whether it has the right colour and light you're after, film it anyway." I was still learning then, and I'm still learning now.

Folk in the film: David Powell-Thompson – award-winning beard

I was with my wife Sue during a weekend in Wasdale when I first met David Powell-Thompson.

As we pulled up outside The Strands Inn, excited about having Sunday dinner and necking a few ales from the microbrewery, another vehicle pulled into the car park and the driver got out and walked into the pub.

"Holy Moses – that's David Powell-Thompson!" I thought. I was aware of David, a mountain guide who had worked on Julia Bradbury's *Wainwright Walks* television series, but had no idea he lived near Wasdale. I didn't say anything to him that day, nor the following day when we returned to The Strands and saw him again.

It was photographer Mark Gilligan who, having done a lot of work with David, thought it would be good to involve him in the Scafell film. Mark suggested we meet over a pint in The Strands. David was wary initially, but we parted on good terms and I sensed there was some interest. By happy coincidence we bumped into each other again in The Strands on each of the following three evenings. We'd have a beer and a natter, and after a short time we clicked. We've been best mates ever since.

David used to be head teacher at St Bega's School in Eskdale, until Eric Robson asked him to help make a series of *Great Walks* videos. That led him into doing research for different programmes, early retirement from teaching and, eventually, working with Julia Bradbury on *Wainwright Walks*. He has a fascinating collection of books about Cumbria and the Lake District – some no longer in print – which he turns to when he can't remember a fact, or when he's looking for something of interest in an area with which he's not familiar.

> David's beard is no ordinary beard – it's an award-winning beard. Every year, before October's Wasdale Show, he manicures its golden locks ready for the Best Beard competition.

David's a lovely, sweet guy and easily recognisable, with his distinctive scraggly ginger hair and beard. It's no ordinary beard, either – it's an award-winning beard. Every year, before October's Wasdale Show, he manicures its golden locks ready for the Best Beard competition. But it's no vanity thing – he's got his eye on the prize; £15 of tokens for the bar – and he's gutted if he doesn't win.

A lot of people are surprised to find that David's in his early 70s: he neither acts nor looks it, and his fell-running achievements are the envy of folk half his age. He only took up the sport when he was 50, while working on a programme about Joss Naylor's renowned 60th birthday run over 60 fells. David started running so he could keep up with Joss during filming, and he's been running ever since. For his own 60th David completed the Joss Naylor Lakeland Challenge – 58 miles and 30 summits – in 15 hours, 54 minutes, and now completes a long run each birthday, finishing back at the maypole in Nether Wasdale. Joss runs onto the fells to meet David and accompany him on the final leg.

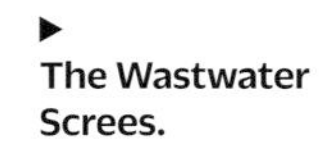

The Wastwater Screes.

◄ The Wasdale Show from Great Gable

▲ Wild camps on Scafell Pike (top) and near Three Tarns (below).

As work on *Scafell Pike* progressed funds dwindled, and I realised I'd not anticipated how much sponsorship money I would need to complete the project.

David and I share many interests, not least wild camping and being out on the fells, and we often share stories while we walk and camp together. Our characters differ – he's more of a pacifist, whereas I can be a bit more brutal about things – but he doesn't stand for nonsense and doesn't like people who are egotistical or narcissistic; something else we have in common.

Working with him is a pleasure. It's easy because we know each other and understand each other's ways. David's not driven by a need to be in front of the camera and finds it amusing how some people lap up the media attention. That said, when he's working behind the bar at The Strands, it makes his day if a customer recognises him from the walking DVDs or one of the *Life of a Mountain* films. He's chuffed to think someone might have learned something from them.

When he appears in the films and DVDs, nothing David says is scripted. We know where we're going to go and the subjects he's going to be talking about, but the rest is down to him. David's been with me throughout the trilogy – he opened and closed *Blencathra* – and, because we know each other so well, his contributions are always captured in one take. Then off we go, ready for the next shoot.

Commercial break: winter in the Cairngorms

As work on *Scafell Pike* progressed, funds dwindled, and I realised I'd not anticipated how much sponsorship money I would need to complete the project. I had not asked for enough seed investment, and the kitty was running low.

So I came up with a plan to make a one-off DVD, which could be sold to generate interim funds. I approached Chris Townsend, one of Britain's most experienced backpackers, who I knew of through his writings in *The Great Outdoors*, and was delighted to find that he knew who I was from my blog and videos. We hit it off immediately and when I outlined my idea – to make a video featuring him in the Cairngorms during winter – he loved it.

I hoped the video would capture the Cairngorm landscape in all its glory, taking the audience on a journey with Chris as their guide on some of his favourite walks. I also hoped to reveal some of his backpacking secrets – how he chooses a campsite, what gear he takes and why – and to convey something of his spiritual nature and of the therapeutic effect the great outdoors can have on your soul.

Chris is something of a hero to me due to the amazing walks he has undertaken. It seems criminal that Chris is not feted more for his pioneering achievements here in the UK. He's walked from Land's End to John O'Groats, and was first to complete a continuous walk over all of Scotland's Munros and Tops. In North America he has walked the Pacific Crest and Continental Divide trails, was first to walk the length of the Canadian Rockies and was one of the first to walk the 1,200-mile Pacific Northwest Trail from the Continental Divide to the Pacific Ocean. His achievements are better appreciated in the US, where he is revered by the hiking community. People in the UK outdoors community might have heard of him, but the public at large don't have a clue.

To get the Cairngorms project off the ground I announced a Kickstarter appeal on my blog, asking people to donate in return for incentives such as digital versions of the finished video, signed prints, DVDs, copies of Chris's recent book *A Year in the Life of the Cairngorms* – even the opportunity to spend time with us during filming. We would both hopefully make a little money from sales which would, in my case, tide me over while I finished *Life of a Mountain: Scafell Pike*. I hoped we could complete the video within a month, but I set aside three months out of *Scafell*'s two-year production cycle – January, February and March 2013 – for the project, which it turned out was just as well.

I had never visited the Cairngorms before and found the scale of the place – and the conditions – daunting. The Cairngorms National Park is twice the size of the Lake District and is Britain's largest area of land over 2,600 feet. It encompasses a range of landscapes, from mountains and alpine-arctic plateaux to ancient Caledonian forest, rocky corries, high passes and remote lochs. In winter the landscape becomes as harsh as it is beautiful, and the conditions I experienced were the most extreme I've met on the hills. The Cairngorms demand solid outdoor skills.

▲▶ **North to the Cairngorms: Chris Townsend (above), and Chris on Ben Macdui (right) – 'The conditions I experienced were the most extreme I've met on the hills.'**

"You'd have died out there... If you'd gone to Corrour Bothy you wouldn't have made it out."

Shouldering the pain

During a filming break in Newark I started to experience some discomfort around the back of my shoulder. I'd had a lump there for a while, which I thought was a swollen cyst or something that would go away of its own accord. But one Sunday afternoon it inflamed to the size of a satsuma. I was due to head back to the Cairngorms within a day or two, so Sue took me to our local A&E. The doctors had a look, figured it was nothing more than an infection and sent me off with some pills.

A few days later Chris and I were back in the Cairngorms, planning to walk over the Lairig Ghru – the mountain pass that climbs above 2,700 feet – to Corrour Bothy. But the weather was so bad on the exposed route that we had to bail out. We ended up camping in Rothiemurchus, quite late in the day. There the pain in my shoulder worsened. I was in agony and the infection felt wet and cold. I took off my top and asked Chris to take a look. He was silent for a few moments, then said: "We need to get you to hospital." The lump had swollen and was leaking blood and pus.

After a sleepless night we walked out the following day, and Chris drove me to the small hospital in Aviemore where a doctor performed surgery on my shoulder under local anaesthetic. He cut a quarter inch into my flesh and removed the source of the problem.

The doctor was a keen mountaineer himself and something of a fan of Chris, who he said had done exactly the right thing in insisting we leave the hill to seek medical attention. I'd been at risk of blood poisoning from the infection, he explained, and if we'd continued to walk in to Corrour Bothy we would have been on the wrong side of the Lairig Ghru to summon help. Chris would not have been able to get a phone signal – even if he had climbed onto one of the surrounding peaks.

"You'd have died out there," he told me, bluntly, as he patched me up. "If you'd gone to Corrour Bothy you wouldn't have made it out."

Afterwards I had some kind of fit, either an allergic reaction to the anaesthetic or belated shock from surgery. I started kicking, smashing things and shouting; I don't remember much other than waking up thirsty and drinking gallons of water. Because of the fit the doctors kept me in longer, until I convinced them to release me to a local guest house.

I had to return to the hospital every day for a week. Thankfully the owners of the guest house waived the fee and even drove me to hospital some days because the pills I'd been given prevented me from walking. The moment I received the all-clear I returned to the mountains and captured more footage of Chris and the peaks, before getting the train home.

I came to regard Chris as a proper friend over those three months – the kind I can talk to about anything and know that it will go no further. I haven't a bad word to say about him. Sometimes, when you read a book or a magazine article, you can hear the author's voice in your head. Well, that's Chris in real life: authoritative, relaxed and honest. I always enjoy meeting up with him. We share some traits too: when we're camping together, we pitch a distance apart; we each like our own space – we're both there for the sense of wilderness and nature, and understand that we don't have to be pitched side by side to appreciate that.

Equally, I'm fond of teasing him. His appearance can be trampy at times, and he likes wearing sandals in the mountains, which I wind him up about: "Chris, cut your toenails, man!" He also suffers from a bad case of early-morning bed-head on wild camps. His face swells up around his eyes until he doesn't look like Chris any more. "Jesus Christ – is that you, Chris?" I also rib him about the awful dried food he eats on camp, which has almost no nutritional content at all. A wild-camp meal for me is proper pasta or three-minute rice, with tuna steaks from a foil pouch and dried vegetables – that's a hearty meal.

The Cairngorms in Winter was my first proper feature-length video. I don't refer to it as a film (it's more a programme with filmic elements to it), but I learned a lot from the experience, both in production terms – what I had to do became much clearer in my mind – and in testing myself in such an extreme environment: those brutal winter storms ensured I was ready to face anything the Scafells could throw at me.

Shooting on a shoestring

During the making of *Life of a Mountain: Scafell Pike*, my equipment was extremely modest. That meant being creative about capturing a particular shot using limited resources. One such shot was the moving time-lapse – where time speeds up and the view shifts slowly across a changing landscape – in the days before I had a computer-managed rail (a track along which a camera moves automatically, firing off pictures as it goes).

When tucked up under the duvet in a bed and breakfast, people lose sight of the fact that the Lake District is not only beautiful during the day, it's beautiful at night too. The shot I wanted was a moving time-lapse capturing the drama of the Lakeland night sky.

▲
Camp on Mullach Clach a'Bhlair, Cairngorms.

When we're camping together, we pitch a distance apart: we each like our own space.

I looked at our kitchen egg timer and wondered if I could stick the GoPro on that.

My GoPro camera was capable of recording time-lapse sequences – I just needed it to turn independently, in short increments so the footage was smooth.

How to do that on no budget? A potential answer came to me when making breakfast. I looked at our kitchen egg timer and wondered if I could stick the GoPro on that. The timer was cylindrical – perfect for mounting the cameras on – and it worked, but only up to a point. I shot some semi-usable footage, but most of the time it wasn't worth the hassle: I couldn't control the speed of the timer as it moved; if I wanted it to go slower I was stuck. It was just one example of me improvising with kit that BBC professionals take for granted.

At other times I learned how to get the most out of the limited kit I had.

All the electronics I carry demand that I take a lot of batteries. They have to be kept warm if they're to keep their charge, especially on cold nights. To preserve their heat I stuff them in the pockets of my down jacket, but the cold mountain environment still dulls them quickly.

If a camera indicates its battery is dying when it should be fully charged, I know it's just the cold. The battery is not really dead – instead it's gone docile. When that happens I swap batteries and get them back up to temperature so the electrons re-fire. I also insulate batteries by wrapping them in my deer stalker hat. Sometimes I use elastic bands to fasten hand-warmers to a device to keep its batteries warm, and I'll wrap spare socks around it, especially during night time-lapse sequences when the camera's running for long periods. Such sequences are hit and miss in winter, as I might be sleeping in my tent while the camera's at work, trusting to luck that it runs smoothly.

▲
Dawn from Cairn Gorm.

▲
Cloud layers above and below Crinkle Crags.

Daytime lapse shoots are easier because I can keep an eye on the equipment.

A camera lens also needs to acclimatise before you can start shooting, otherwise it mists over. If it's cold enough, frost can even form on the glass. When a camera's been in my sleeping bag to keep the battery warm the lens will fog as soon as it meets the cold air outside. The same principle is at work when you walk into a warm pub from the cold: you get a runny nose and your glasses instantly steam up.

A better solution to the challenge posed by battery chill and foggy lenses, I've found, is to leave the cameras in the cold tent porch during the night and stash batteries in my sleeping bag with me.

Back to A&E

On completing filming for the Cairngorms DVD, I returned to Newark in desperate need of a haircut. My hair was everywhere – I'd spent so long with Chris Townsend I was starting to look like him! One winter's day I paid a visit to my barber and walked out afterwards to find it was starting to snow.

Then I was overcome by the strangest sensation.

A snowflake hit my lip and, within moments, my mouth started to drool and my face began to sag. Over the next five minutes it felt like something was travelling from my lip, very slowly down to my neck, into my shoulder, then all the way down my arm to a point where I could feel it going through every finger on my right hand. It felt like part of my face had gone numb; suddenly I couldn't do anything with my arm. I thought I must be having a stroke. Sheltering under a market stall, I dialled 999 and described my symptoms. The next thing I knew I was off to hospital, though to this day I can't remember whether I went in an ambulance or walked.

The NHS was brilliant. My arteries were immediately given an ultrasound scan, after which I was told I could leave for the evening as long as Sue was with me. They warned me not to get straight up and rush out, but, thinking I felt OK, I did exactly what they'd advised against, and felt dreadful. Sue had to help me out.

A snowflake hit my lip and, within moments, my mouth started to drool and my face began to sag... Sheltering under a market stall, I dialled 999.

▲
Kit laid out inside Terry's tent.

Over the next four or five days I was given every assessment imaginable. The hospital staff were thorough: I was put through the full gamut, including an MRI on my brain and countless blood tests – I thought I wasn't going to have any blood left at the rate they were taking it out – as the doctors were concerned that I might have had a transient ischemic attack (TIA), an interruption in the flow of blood to the brain. Its symptoms – including the weakness I had experienced down the side of my body – match those of a stroke. But I passed all the tests; the doctors found nothing wrong with my brain, my arteries were fine and I was told – again – that my heart was strong as that of an ox.

When I returned for the final test results, a specialist confirmed that it had been a TIA, maybe caused by a blood clot – though no one could tell me what might have caused a clot. I was lucky it hadn't done any damage and fortunate that it had happened after we'd finished filming the Cairngorms DVD, because if it had happened on the fell it would have meant another trip to Aviemore hospital – and one that's unlikely to have had a happy ending.

I took the opportunity to ask the specialist what, in his opinion, might have caused the health scare I'd had three years earlier. He examined my records and suspected the cause could have been a calcium deficiency in my diet. That surprised me: like most people, I associate calcium with bones and teeth, but he explained it also plays a role in the cardiac system: if we don't get enough calcium the heart doesn't work properly.

The latest tests had also shown that my cholesterol levels were sky-high – high enough to put me at risk of a potentially fatal heart attack. It wasn't due to a particularly unhealthy diet, but more my irregular eating patterns. When camping out I would eat generally healthy food and my body would start fasting. Returning from the hills, however, I'd carb-binge on McDonald's and other junk before getting back into a healthier eating regime, so my weight and cholesterol levels were constantly fluctuating. The doctor said he was not going to prescribe statins: partly because I hadn't reached the age when they tend to be prescribed, but also because they can have harmful long-term side effects. Anyway, he said, he knew me well enough to trust me to adopt a healthy diet.

The news was a relief, though I had one outstanding question. I'd been honest with him about absolutely everything – including my penchant for ale. Had the tests revealed, I tentatively asked, whether there was anything wrong with my liver?

"Above-average health."

"I can continue drinking beer?"

"Sure," he replied. In fact my drinking habits, he said, had probably helped lessen the effects of the TIA: I never mix drinks, I don't binge and I don't like getting drunk.

I left the doctors resolving to eat better from that day forward.

Just as soon as I'd been to the pub and had one last McDonald's, of course.

I resolved to eat better from that day forward. Just as soon as I'd been to the pub and had one last McDonald's, of course.

Return to Scafell Pike

Chris and I enjoyed each other's company so much in the Cairngorms that I invited him to take part in *Scafell Pike*. He liked the idea because many of his early big walks had been in the Lakes. And I liked the idea because Chris speaks my language – the language of backpacking and wild camping. Backpacking – the practice of disappearing into the hills carrying everything you need for a few days – is how I connect with nature and the landscape. Chris's inclusion in the film made it easier for me to convey, through him, the reasons why I head into the wilds and why I find it so fulfilling.

When backpacking, you get to see sights few others see – sunsets, sunrises, dawn inversions, stars at night... the essence of what I sought to include in the film. I enjoy a range of outdoor activities, including walking and mountain biking, but when wild camping I connect with the fells in a deeper, more spiritual way that is good for the soul. I see the fells in a different light and feel more in tune with the landscape around me. Everything I wanted to share with the audience was channelled through Chris's love of wild camping.

I chose Upper Eskdale for my shoot with Chris because it retains a strong sense of wilderness – you rarely encounter anybody else there, and it offers a majestic view of the Scafells, particularly in winter. From the Wasdale side the Scafells look like large grassy hills with craggy knobs, but from Upper Eskdale they look like mountains proper. Even though it's not true wilderness country, Chris was able to convey the sense of wilderness that can be experienced there.

I'd hoped the backpacking scene could be shot in snow as I'd planned to include it in the winter section of the film, but the weather wasn't behaving when we set out and, although it was winter, everything had an autumnal hue.

Then, overnight, we were blessed with mountain magic... Upon waking, the upland bowl of Great Moss was white with fresh snow. I hadn't planned to film that morning, but some scenes demand to be shot, so I set to work and afterwards, instead of packing up, I dumped the kit and we walked off into the snow to enjoy the moment. That scene conveys just what it's like to camp in winter.

On the heels of a legend

Joss Naylor is a fell-running legend. Someone once described him as the greatest Olympian who's never taken part in the Olympics. His litany of fell-running achievements might never be bettered: he held the record for running the Wainwrights for 27 years; the record for the Welsh 3,000s and for the Pennine Way, each for 15 years; and has held numerous Bob Graham records, including running more than 100 miles over 72 peaks in less than 24 hours.

I'd wanted to include Joss in *Scafell Pike*, but although I had a rough idea he lived in Wasdale, I didn't know exactly where.

Sue came up to help me while I was working on the film and we stayed in a Wasdale holiday cottage for a few summer nights. One morning I looked out of the cottage window – it was early, about three or four o'clock – and I could see there would be a nice sunrise. Leaving Sue asleep, I grabbed the camera and legged it up the fell behind the cottage in my jimjams. As I was filming, I heard a whistle or two, and thought: "Bugger! Someone's around, and here

▶ **Great End and Great Gable.**

▲ **Sedbergh shepherdess Alison O'Neill, who bookends both *Scafell Pike* and *Helvellyn*.**

I am in my jimjams." Then I saw it was Joss, out giving his dog a run. I waited until he went home before running inside to get changed.

Later I went round and knocked on the door of the cottage he'd gone into, but he was out. I asked about him in The Strands that night and someone gave me his phone number, so I called him up. A few days later I went back to Joss's cottage and filmed the interview that appears in the documentary, then spent a few hours grabbing footage of him out on the fell. As we set off, he told his wife Mary he'd be back by dinner time for his sandwich. Joss was in his late 70s the day I met him but was still – and remains today – extremely fit. He might not look so at first glance, but once we were out on the fell I struggled to keep up. It wasn't the first or last time during filming I was reminded never to judge a book by its cover.

> Wasdale remains heaven to Joss. He will always be part of the geology of the valley – part of the cultural fabric of that perfect pocket of Lakeland.

It was gone two o'clock before we got back. Joss opened the door very sheepishly; Mary was not at all happy that he was late for his sandwich. I muttered: "Sorry Mrs Naylor," bundled up my wires and chargers and shuffled out into the street to pack my equipment away.

I don't think Joss's fell-running achievements will ever be topped – certainly not in my lifetime. When he was a youngster he had operations on his knee and his back, so there's an argument to say that because he's at a physiological disadvantage to other fell-runners he shouldn't be running at all. But he has never let it hold him back and I suppose that's testament to his stamina – and to the drive and passion he has inside him.

I still visit Joss from time to time. He no longer lives at the head of the valley, and spends winters in Spain, but you'll still see him at Wasdale Shepherd's Meet each year. The valley remains heaven to him. It offers him everything that floats his boat, and to me, Joss will always be part of the geology of Wasdale – part of the cultural fabric of that perfect pocket of Lakeland.

Follower of fashions

It was only when I was into the second year of the film's production, while working on some edits, that I realised I didn't have anyone to introduce and close the documentary. I'd not given these end points any thought until then – in fact I'd not even been sure they would be right for the film.

I cast around for ideas, and one of my contacts at the National Trust suggested I might talk to Sedbergh shepherdess Alison O'Neill.

I was aware of Alison, having read about her in various outdoor magazines. A qualified walking leader as well as a consummate hill farmer, she cuts a striking figure in the iconic tweed clothing that she designs herself and is woven from wool clipped from her own rough fell, Swaledale and Herdwick flocks. She has a reputation for promoting the benefits of barefoot walking on the fells, encouraging walkers to experience the feel of the earth beneath their soles and fresh water running between their toes. Though the Scafells aren't her patch, her family had farmed in Cumbria for many years. Even before meeting her I knew she'd be perfect to bookend the film.

I wanted to meet her first, to find out how she came across, because that's important whether you're filming someone or watching them on a screen. She's quite the romantic, and her enthusiasm for what she does, and for the landscape, is infectious. We got on like a house on fire.

Man of the mountains

Over the course of the two years it took to make *Scafell Pike*, a sort of routine developed, shaped around wild-camp trips onto the fells that would last for six, seven and sometimes more nights at a time. To resupply I'd pop down to the valley to collect food, grab a shower, enjoy a beer and recharge my batteries – literally and figuratively.

In winter, Sue would order Asda and Tesco deliveries, which the folk who lived at the Wasdale Head Inn would accept and store in the fridge for me until I descended the fell to collect it. They knew to expect me at two or three in the afternoon: I'd turn up dishevelled, in need of a shave and a wash, stuff the new supplies into my pack and head out again next morning. While I was at the inn they'd let me connect to wi-fi so I could contact Sue and let her know I was alive and well.

There were times when the weather was so

I came to recognise certain rocks, patches of moss, specific clumps of moorland grass. When the snows came I knew where the cornices would build – even in white-out conditions.

wild that it wasn't safe to be on the tops; then, I'd have to stay down in the valley. It wasn't always practical to use a campsite: I was on foot, carrying a load that might weigh as much as 75kg, and I didn't want to have to trudge six or seven valley-bottom miles to a site, only to have to retrace them in the morning to return onto the fell. Instead I'd camp in beer gardens or farmers' fields – as long as I was behind a wall out of sight from the public.

As filming progressed I grew to know the fells, and the localised patch I was filming on, intimately. The only people who knew the territory better than me were a few shepherds and guidebook authors like Mark Richards. They, however, would only be out periodically, and in certain conditions, whereas as I found myself out continuously, and in all weathers.

As my knowledge of the fells improved, I came to refer to my well-worn maps less frequently. Even when it was clagged in and visibility was poor I knew where I was: I came to recognise certain rocks, patches of moss, specific clumps of moorland grass. When the snows came I knew where the cornices would build, even in white-out conditions. I knew where the screes started and the mountain ended. In heat waves I knew where the springs would still flow, and as time passed I developed a shortlist of special camping spots – discreet, unfrequented places where I could set up a base camp and leave the tent pitched for a few nights while filming. Even today, I rarely use a map and compass in the Scafells.

Any port in a storm

In winter I would carry a 100-litre rucksack with a load that might weigh somewhere between 70–75kg. Rucksacks with that kind of capacity are like hens' teeth these days, but the pack needed to be big enough to hold everything for several nights – not just my camping equipment, but also microphones, cameras, lenses and spare clothes. I would save weight on stuff others might consider essentials: evening clothes, books, home comforts. I lived the life of a wayfarer, carrying gas and food but not water, which I collected from springs. My one luxury was booze: on some trips I would take beers – if I couldn't be in the pub, I'd take the pub with me. On others I would fill my two-litre Platypus with port, which I'd polish off over four or five hours. If I was out for a few nights I'd stagger it.

There were times, though, when the physical and psychological demands were so tough they left me struggling. During one multi-night expedition into Upper Eskdale, I yomped over the open fell for miles in horrible conditions. There was no path to walk on and I was battling the weather, getting increasingly tired. That evening, the tent finally set up, I sat in the porch as the weather blew a hoolie outside and started to cry uncontrollably, for no reason I could understand. I wasn't sad, I wasn't in pain, and I came to realise the tears were my body telling me to: "Slow down; you're exhausted, you need to rest."

I was missing home too. Being away for weeks at a time was hard on both me and on Sue back home. Stuck in the same damp tent, sometimes with frost forming on the inside, and sick of freeze-dried meals, I felt increasingly isolated and lonely. I had to resist thoughts of slipping back to a warm home. I'd take trinkets with me – little reminders of home that became coping mechanisms. Sue had given me a fluffy hat one Christmas, which I used during my winter camps. A drink, meanwhile, helped me wind down from the physical exhaustion, knocking me out and helping to bring on sleep.

These long trips on the fells were tough, both mentally and physically. But when the sun broke over the horizon and I could capture the soft-changing dawn colours on the fells, my mood would change in an instant. Then I'd be buzzing – high as a kite. I would spend days, weeks on the fells, to capture the precious few seconds in which I got the shots that mattered.

But there was reward, too, during the tough times: in the wild winds, the bitter cold, the waist-deep snows. The challenges are tests that bring perspective to life, that build character, so that everyday worries are reduced to nothing. You come out of them stronger and better able to appreciate the small things in life: central heating, an oven, a warm pub... a decent pint.

One for the album

Backpackers who love the Lakes will know there's nowhere to camp on the summit of Bowfell. It's solid rock. One of my most memorable camps, however, took place there in the depths of a full-monty winter when the snow was so deep camping was easy.

I had been after a distant winter shot of the Scafells over the gulf of Great Moss – I wanted golden light on the snow, dark moody skies above – and my perseverance looked set to pay off that following morning as I emerged from the tent into a raging gale with high-level cloud. The far horizon was clear, and the sun was just breaking through the gap, illuminating the cloud above and streaking out onto the fells. It was one of those rare landscape filming days when all the boxes were ticked.

While checking my pockets I saw this vision of my tent silhouetted against the sun with my ice axe next to it, the sky on fire.

The air temperature was probably something like -2°C or -3°C. I checked the wind chill – it was -20°C, a measure of how strong the winds were. I looked back to my tent, while checking my pockets to see that I had everything I needed, and at that moment saw this vision of my tent, silhouetted against the sun with my ice axe next to it, the sky on fire.

"That's a shot I really ought to take as a momento," I thought... But that would involve the hassle of retrieving the camera from my pack in the raging wind. "Do I? Don't I? Ah, what the hell..." So I threw the pack down, dug the camera out and fired a couple of pictures off, then legged it to the summit.

I got the footage of the Scafells I was after

▲ **Wild camp on Bowfell.**

▶ **Winter dawn from Bowfell. "One of those rare landscape filming days when all the boxes were ticked."**

from Bowfell, but only by clinging onto the tripod to prevent the camera from being blown over. As the sun rose higher and disappeared behind cloud, the perfect conditions waned. I packed up my tent and headed off to Langdale and the Old Dungeon Ghyll.

I used two clips from that footage in the film's closing sequence, as well as a still on the cover of the DVD. But it was the reaction to the photograph of my tent that took me by surprise. I had thought little of it at the time – it was a personal souvenir – but it went viral, appearing in a number of magazines and websites.

Storm on Harter Fell

"If you're on Harter Fell you need to get off."

I was camped just down from the summit rocks on a beautiful winter's day, looking forward to capturing material at sunset, when the text came through. There was a dusting of snow around, but a friend was warning me there was a hellish storm coming in – 70, 80 miles-per-hour winds minimum.

I had a view out across the Irish Sea, but could see no sign of a storm. I asked him if he was sure. "Yeah, about midnight," he texted back. Reluctantly, I took down the tent, moved a short distance from the summit and, based on what he was telling me about the likely wind direction, re-pitched in the lee of a boulder outcrop.

Sure enough, by midnight the tent was being pushed flush to my face by a relentless gale. As the wind strengthened, the poles started bending and buckling into all sorts of shapes. I don't know how the canvas survived. Some people might have bailed out, but I figured I was warm, I was dry – why risk being blown off a fell in the middle of nowhere in the dark? So I decided to sit it out and try for some sleep.

The storm was still blowing a hoolie at first light. I realised I had to plan very carefully if I was going to get the tent down and everything

▲ **Approaching storm, Ulpha.**

◄ **First light over the Scafells.**

As the wind strengthened, the poles started bending and buckling into all sorts of shapes. I don't know how the canvas survived.

packed away without kit blowing away. Crawling through the snow on my hands and knees, working virtually blind, I pulled up the pegs then rolled across the tent fabric to stop the gale taking it. I packed kit into the rucksack to ensure it was heavy enough not to blow off the crag. I couldn't wait to get off the fell.

Thinking that my next two days' filming were out of the window, I retreated to Eskdale, yomping down the valley for miles as I looked for somewhere to stay for the night. Eventually I found a cheap B&B from where I was able to

Gripping my ice axe for dear life while kicking my crampons into the snow, I skidded to a halt just ten feet from a clifftop drop into Upper Eskdale.

call Sue and beg her for a credit card number to cover food and accommodation. I promised her it was for just one night; I'd be back out again as soon as the storm had passed.

I was careful to ask, though, for a little extra money on top for a decent beer.

Slip-sliding away

Conditions were poor and deteriorating as I set off up Brown Tongue from Wasdale. The tops were still plastered in snow and people had voiced concern that I was planning to camp high. The following morning's weather, however, was due to improve and so, determined to capture shots of dawn light striking the war memorial summit cairn, I changed my plan: instead of pitching on Lingmell I gambled on heading onwards to the Pike itself.

It was an arduous ascent, wading through snow that was fast turning to slush. I hoped to arrive just after sunset, pitch, then endure whatever the weather threw at me overnight to get my sunrise shots. I reached Mickledore in fading light and pea-soup visibility.

I'd just passed the mountain rescue stretcher box when I plunged into a waist-deep snowdrift. A combination of momentum, my heavy pack and the pull of gravity began to drag me through the snow until I was sliding head-first, on my back, down the slope towards a sheer edge. What happened next remains a blur – I remember thinking fleetingly I was going to die – but I somehow managed to get my head facing up the fell, then rolled onto my side and, gripping my ice axe for dear life while kicking my crampons into the snow, I skidded to a halt just ten feet from a clifftop drop into Upper Eskdale.

I sat puffing and panting in the snow for about 20 minutes, lighting a cigarette to calm my nerves. It was getting dark and I cursed, asking myself what the hell I was doing. "I could have died here and no-one would have known until they found my body days later. Picked the wrong day to quit smoking," I thought.

Gradually, however, I came around and thought: "I'm alive, I'm alright, and I've got two litres of port that'll drown out the nightmares." So I picked myself up and ploughed – literally – on to the summit. Conditions there were no better; the wind raged and the snow was so deep my axe didn't touch rock. I spent half an hour kicking away snow and stamping the surface flat to give me a platform for the tent and to keep the snow pegs more rigid. When I finally pitched and crawled inside, out of the wind, it felt luxurious. I drank my port, slept

▲ **Stanley Force, Eskdale.**

▶ **Summer dawn, Glaramara.**

I'd become so familiar with my little patch of the Western Lakes that there was a danger of complacency creeping in.

▲
'You get this finished and I'll loan you the money': Eric Robson.

like a baby, and when I woke at dawn the sun was out and there was drama in the clouds. The shots I captured – which form part of the film's closing scene – made it all worthwhile.

Steady as you go

I told Sue about the slide sometime after I'd returned to Newark. I always tell her about these things, though not at the time as I don't want her to worry. She was mortified, of course – she thinks I'm crazy.

Like many mountain folk, I learn from these kinds of brushes with danger then hide them away in my memory and try not to let them bother me again. If you don't do that, you can easily get messed up. This near-death incident, however, had a more profound impact on how I approached the fells. Since then, faced with similar conditions, I've bailed out. My new way of thinking says: "If I persevere, the chances that my life might end today are greater; if I pull back, I'm increasing the likelihood of seeing another day."

Most people exercise care when they find themselves in an unfamiliar environment, but I'd become so familiar with my little patch of the Western Lakes that there was a danger of complacency creeping in. Accidents happen when you develop that kind of attitude. And on the winter fells you need to be extra careful – nervous, even. Being on edge is what keeps you alive.

In these conditions I now find myself consciously alert, thinking: "Where can I place my feet? Is that snow alright there? I don't recognise that hump – could it be a mini cornice?" On the safe, wider and flat parts of the fell I'll yomp along; elsewhere I take shorter steps, take my time and never rush – that's when you're likely to trip and fall. In winter conditions a broken ankle can be as deadly as a 200-foot fall.

The big 100-litre pack, which contributed to my near-miss fall, has on other occasions been a lifesaver. Logically, you'd think it would be destabilising, but at times it has had the opposite effect, cushioning me when I've fallen and steadying me against strong winds.

The funds run low

One winter's evening in 2015 I was in the Santon Bridge Inn with David Powell-Thompson and a few locals, and I was drowning my sorrows.

With three months to go until I was due to finish *Scafell Pike*, I was down to my last £300. I had barely enough left to cover the cost of my return rail tickets. The film's financing had, until now, come from sponsors, the Indiegogo crowd funding, Sue, and from my own pocket. I'd also leant heavily on credit cards. But the funds were pretty much done. I couldn't see a solution.

In the pub with us that evening was broadcaster, author and Wasdale local Eric Robson, known to many Lakes lovers for the series of programmes he made with guidebook author Alfred Wainwright. I'd been introduced to him by David a few months earlier over a pint in the Santon Bridge. I'd been somewhat in awe because of the work he'd done with Wainwright and his role on Radio 4's *Gardeners' Question Time*, but we became friends. I kept him up to speed on the film's progress with short clips on my phone. Noticing that I was troubled he took me to one side and asked what the problem was. I explained I was down to my last £300, my cards were maxed out and there was nothing else coming in.

He asked how much I thought it would take to complete the film. When I told him, he replied: "You get this film finished, and I'll loan you the money – pay me back when you start selling the DVDs."

I told him it was a kind thought, and I appreciated the offer, but I didn't have the money to press any discs either. That was when he mentioned Striding Edge, the DVD production and distribution business he ran with his wife, Annette.

"I'll print the discs – you can pay me back out of royalties. Nothing like *Life of a Mountain* has ever been done before – this film is going to change your life."

A few days later the money arrived in my bank account and, thanks to Eric, I was able to return to the fell.

Strangers in the mist

Pitched in an obscure, off-trail spot at Hollow Stones, high above Wasdale Head, I woke to find myself pinned down by winter weather. I'd planned to head on to the summit of the Pike to shoot gnarly footage of hoarfrost and spindrift, but the fell was socked in with clag – I could only just make out Mickledore – so I decided to sit tight until the weather showed signs of improvement. I put on a coffee and made myself breakfast.

As ever, I'd pitched out of sight of the main paths, so I was surprised when a young couple walked out of the mist and came right up to the tent. In their mid-to-late 20s, they were dressed in the most fashionable walking kit I'd seen, but they didn't have ice axes or crampons and they were carrying the tiniest daypacks you can imagine.

I greeted them with a friendly "Hello", but they walked on by without replying. Why on earth, I wondered, had they come to the tent? They were now ploughing through deep snow among hidden boulders, seemingly unaware of where the paths lay and oblivious to the avalanche debris around them. I called out as they snaked their way towards Mickledore, but the wind must have prevented them from hearing me.

Conditions were still bad when I started my ascent of Scafell Pike's summit. I got as far as Lingmell Col before giving up, and instead turned back a short distance to shelter among boulders and capture shots of Great Gable. Then out of the mist, I saw a figure with a familiar gait coming towards me.

"Alright, Terry? Thought you'd be up here!" It was my mate, landscape photographer Stewart Smith. Stewart's the real deal: one of the few photographers – Mark Littlejohn's another – who gets out onto the fells at all times, in all weathers, to capture true mountain scenes. Stewart and I sheltered together, chatting. He'd got to the top but been frustrated by the weather. When I asked about the young couple, he said he'd been alone up there. Given the conditions, that wasn't surprising, but where had they ended up, I wondered? Mystery unresolved, Stewart made his way down the fell and I returned to Hollow Stones to prep the camera for some night time-lapse shots. With the camera and tripod set up, I returned through the 50-mile-an-hour winds to the tent to make scran and await nightfall.

▲
Pike o'Blisco dawn.

Peering out towards Scafell Crag, the fellside suddenly lit up before returning, just as fast, to black. It happened again and again. "That's

▲
Eskdale Needle in winter.

some powerful torch," I thought. "There's only one group I know with torches that powerful." And it wasn't long before I heard the voices of Wasdale Mountain Rescue Team members, who were working their way around the foot of Scafell, up towards Mickledore and Lingmell. They seemed to be coming from every direction.

After about an hour, two team members came over to the tent. They'd guessed it was me and jokingly asked if they could join me for food and shelter. They could hardly stand in the wind, so knelt in the snow as they asked if I'd seen anybody out.

I described the couple from earlier.

"That's who we're looking for." They'd phoned 999 to request help after becoming lost in dire conditions. As we chatted, a call came over their radio to spread word that duty team leader Mike Gullen had found the couple near the summit. He'd waded through waist-deep snow to get close to them, then thrown a rope because they were sheltered against a cornice. The lads headed off towards Lingmell to help Mike and other team members bring down the couple, who were by then hypothermic.

When the descending party reached Hollow Stones I went over for a chinwag. I even said hello to the couple – but again they didn't respond.

Mike took me to one side, away from the couple and out of the wind.

"You do realise," he said, "they're not going to say hello to you? They'll think you're a nut job in your tent, happy as Larry, while they've had the most frightening experience of their life!" He then asked for a favour. "Will you come off the fell tomorrow? If you want to stay tonight, stay, but come off in the morning because the storm's due to worsen."

I agreed, silently cursing the fact that my time-lapse shot had been ruined.

I included Mike, team president Bill Pattison MBE and their fellow Wasdale Mountain Rescue Team members in the film, first at Wasdale Shepherd's Meet, then out training on the fells, as well as discussing some of the particular pressures they face, such as national Three Peaks challengers coming unstuck on Scafell Pike. Bill put across an important message about over-reliance on mobile phones and other technology on the fells.

The members of Lakeland's 12 rescue teams are the people who mop us up when we come unstuck on the fells. They're all volunteers – everyday folk who interrupt their jobs and personal lives to help others, without judgement or prejudice. They are an essential emergency service, but one the taxpayer doesn't fund. Instead they rely on us throwing coins into tins.

They do a fantastic job – one most of us will never fully grasp or appreciate – and they deserve wider recognition. Their slot in the film gives a little insight into how they go about doing what they do. Time constraints prevented me including as much from the hours of footage I shot as I wanted: I would love to have included Mike Gullen's guided tour of the team's Wasdale base, describing some of the kit they

▲ **Sunrise from Scafell Pike.**

use, and explaining the expense and training time involved in keeping the team operational. Deleted scenes were included on a bonus DVD received by those who crowd-funded the film.

Keeping it real

One of the opening shots in the Scafell film shows an inversion. The Helvellyn range is rising above an ocean of cloud as the sun climbs into the sky, causing high-level cloud to glow a dense range of pinks and oranges. It only lasts for a few seconds. I was the only person on top of Scafell Pike that December morning in 2012 to capture the inversion, and I'll never forget it.

When I posted the images on social media, however, some wags insisted it was faked. The accusation really got my back up; I take pride in that fact that all my fell footage is the real deal. There's no digital trickery – I don't even use post-production filters. I'd taken a picture on my phone, and another on my DSLR while filming, so I posted the three alongside each other in a social media post – phone, DSLR, video footage – to demonstrate that what I'd shot was real. Anyone could witness similar scenes on a given day, in a given season, in given weather conditions.

Which is not to say that anyone else *would* capture the same images.

I have this theory that with my art background – the painting and drawing – I have an eye for a good shot. But whereas with a drawing or painting I *create* the shot – I'm in control of the light and the composition – with landscape video and photography, it's about *capturing* a scene, and that's a different challenge altogether. I can't just wave a wand to throw lovely light and dramatic clouds onto the fells: I have to know in advance what I want to capture and the weather conditions that might help create the perfect image. Most of all, I have to be out there to shoot it when the stars align.

When people ask about capturing the perfect shot I always say there's no magic: it's simply a matter of being in the right place at the right time – with a little luck thrown in.

But by understanding a bit about weather systems, about geography, and about where the sun will rise and set – by properly immersing yourself in the outdoors – you can improve that luck.

The première

As I hunkered down to make the first edit of *Scafell Pike* I realised it could easily end up being a lengthy epic. This didn't worry me – I'm old school: I enjoy longer movies like *Dances with Wolves* and *Lord of the Rings*, in which the producers take their time and, in doing so, create and convey a mood. But that's just me. I worried other people might find *Scafell* laborious – boring, even.

So I was stunned by the reaction when it finally played at its Rheged première in May 2015 before a full house. The audience went nuts. The DVDs flew out, and they've been flying out ever since.

At the première, just when I was starting to feel confident about the public reaction to my film, someone threw a curveball at me during the question-and-answers session: "What does Joss Naylor think of it?"

I was stumped for a moment.

Then I looked round the room. "Well, as it happens, he's here in the audience," I was able to reply.

Joss was sat among the rows near the front, so I asked him, rather sheepishly: "Alright Joss, what did you think of it?"

The audience fell silent. "Aye, lad," he replied. "It were fucking brilliant." The screening room erupted with laughter, and everyone cheered. I had to hold back the tears.

Eric's prediction, that *Life of a Mountain* would change my life had been spot on. Everything changed after that night – and especially after it was shown in edited form on BBC4.

Suddenly I was inundated with suggestions about who I should speak to next – "Here's their email, here's their number, this is their address" – and people were lining up to appear in future projects. For the first time I had the luxury of choice. That was useful: for the trilogy's next instalments if I had an idea to cover a particular subject, someone might now direct me to the right person.

My financial struggles were also a thing of the past thanks to the support of friends, the faith that people had invested in me, and the overwhelming support of the public. I look back on *Scafell Pike* not just in terms of how positively it was received, but as a defining point in my life.

Not that there was time to hang up the pack and rest the boots for long: TV companies, fans and magazine editors were already asking when I'd be starting on the next film in my proposed trilogy.

So it was that my eyes turned north, to that last great bastion of Lakeland mountains before the Scottish border, and to the rocky cliffs of Blencathra.

> I have to know in advance what I want to capture and the weather conditions that might help create the perfect image – and most of all I have to be out there to capture it when the stars align.

▲
Autumn sunset over the Dodds.

PART THREE

BLENCATHRA

THAT EVENING, FROM MY CAMP ON SOUTHER FELL, I PUT WORD OUT ON SOCIAL MEDIA THAT I HAD STARTED WORK ON THE NEXT *LIFE OF A MOUNTAIN* FILM AND THAT ITS TITLE WOULD BE *BLENCATHRA*. FOR THE SECOND TIME IN A MONTH, MY SOCIAL MEDIA FEEDS CAUGHT FIRE.

◄
'God beams' over Castlerigg.

Strike while the fell's for sale...

On New Year's Day, 2015 Sue and I were enjoying a break in Wasdale funded by royalties from sales of the *Life of a Mountain: Scafell Pike* DVD. I was catching up with old friends in the area and dropped in on Eric Robson.

Eric was one of only a few people who were aware at the time that I had been working on an edited cut of *Scafell*, which was due to air on BBC4 within a few weeks.

I had been working on the edit with BBC editor Tony Lazzerini for two months. Preparing a production for broadcast involved a steep learning curve, as successive schedule changes saw the film cut from its original two hours to 90 minutes – then to just one hour.

The documentary department had insisted that as many elements as possible from the full film should be retained, but with just 60 minutes to play with that wasn't feasible, and I'd kept quiet about the broadcast on social media for the simple reason that I hated the edited version. Inevitably, special moments were cut, along with mountain sequences I'd spent months capturing. The many compromises gave it a feel more akin to an extended trailer than a documentary. I didn't think anyone would watch it. Those who did, I feared, would think it awful.

Eric, however, whose company Striding Edge had manufactured and distributed the DVDs for me, was confident that the broadcast edit would prove popular. Knowing that *Scafell* was to be the first in a trilogy, Eric encouraged me to seize the momentum and start on the next *Life of a Mountain* film as soon as possible.

I didn't share Eric's enthusiasm. I was still reeling from spending two years on Scafell and was eager to take time off. I wanted to work on other projects – to bring in some much-needed money – and there was a bigger practical point: I still wasn't sure which fell I wanted the second instalment to focus on. Helvellyn remained my first pick, followed by Blencathra and Skiddaw together.

Eric argued that I should tackle Blencathra instead, leaving Helvellyn to last. Helvellyn, he reasoned, with its rock scenery and drama, was too similar to the Scafells, and for that reason I should tackle something different.

But there was a second reason to favour Blencathra: the iconic northern fell had found itself unwittingly thrust into the public limelight. Seven months earlier, Hugh, the eighth Earl of Lonsdale, Viscount Lowther, Baron of Whitehaven and Lord of the Manor of Threlkeld, had put the mountain on the market to pay off a £9 million inheritance tax bill following the death of his father, James Lowther, in 2006. In response, two groups had formed on social media – Buy Blencathra on

Twitter, and Friends of Blencathra on Facebook – to try to raise the £1.75 million asking price and save the fell in perpetuity for the nation. The mountain was topical, Eric insisted, and I needed to strike while the iron was hot.

I wasn't so sure. I needed time and space to think about where the films went next.

The feeds go nuts

On the evening of Tuesday 13 January my social media feeds went nuts. Simultaneously, hundreds of emails flooded my inbox. Moments earlier, a feature about my work on the Scafells film – due to be broadcast in edited form on BBC4 the following evening – had appeared on BBC One's *Inside Out*.

The response knocked me for six. My social media followers were also sharing press previews of *Scafell* that had appeared in *The Times*, *The Guardian* and others, all raving about the film. *The Guardian* – which made it 'Pick of the Day' – declared that it had "a touch of the art-house classic *Koyaanisqatsi*" about it, and said it was "a tribute to the backpackers, mountain guides and rescue teams who traverse those gorgeous slopes", while the *Radio Times* named it 'Documentary of the Week', declaring it "a plain and simple, knock-'em-dead nature" documentary.

I nearly fell off my seat. This was the BBC edit – the one I thought a far cry from my original vision. What did I know? Besides, these were just pre-broadcast previews: the wider public had to watch the film and like it before I could regard it as a hit.

And then it was a hit. A big hit. Viewing figures were just a smidge under a million – a record for a BBC4 programme in its time slot, even before the addition of iPlayer figures. It was the eighth most popular programme of the evening, beating even Bear Grylls' big-budget ITV show.

Overnight, I found myself on the radar of a lot of people, including a number of household names who started following me online. While on a wild camping trip around Wasdale I received private messages from a gentleman saying how much he loved my Lake District pictures, and that he always followed where I was camped. After a week or two I recognised the name – *Top Gear*'s Richard Hammond. There was musician Gary Kemp, and radio presenter Stuart Maconie, who in turn told me comedian Steve Coogan was a fan of *Scafell*.

Eric's suggestion that things would change with the nationwide viewing of *Scafell* proved right, and pressure was building for me to commit to a second film. But I still hadn't

▲ Sunbreak, Clough Head.

◄ Blencathra from a frosty Castlerigg Stone Circle.

Overnight, I found myself on the radar of a lot of people, including a number of household names.

untangled the questions I had over where to shoot. To get things straight in my head I took myself off for a camp on Souther Fell, a subsidiary top of Blencathra, to chill out, relax, and think about where my trilogy should head next.

It was a dramatic evening, with a strengthening wind rattling the tent overnight. I got some nice shots on a new camera bought with proceeds from *Scafell*, and when I reviewed the footage I realised I'd been bitten by the film bug again. I was ready. I also realised that Eric was right: Blencathra was the perfect subject for the next *Life of a Mountain* film. But it would be Blencathra alone: it's an icon in its own right and combining it with Skiddaw, as I'd originally planned, would not do it justice. Helvellyn – more my kind of fell – would become the trilogy's finale.

That evening, from my camp on Souther Fell, I put word out on social media that I had started work on the next *Life of a Mountain* and that its title would be *Blencathra*. For the second time in a month, my feeds caught fire. I started receiving emails and calls from TV stations, local journalists and others, all wanting to know more about the forthcoming film.

"Holy crap," I thought. "No pressure!"

'Second album' trick

The *Scafell* showing on BBC4 was a game-changer. Suddenly I was earning decent royalties – money that until now I'd only dreamt about. Unlike in my old party days, I didn't piss it up the wall. After I'd paid off debts and bills all the cash was channelled straight into supporting me during the making of *Blencathra*. I was seeking sponsorship again, but the fact that my own money was going into the project was an incentive to ensure I did a good job – and to enable me to pull off that difficult 'second album' trick.

I began to think through how the film might start and finish, and what unfulfilled ambitions for *Scafell* I could bring to *Blencathra*. This would be helped by the fact that I could now afford to upgrade some of my equipment. For *Scafell Pike*, I'd used a bottom-end, pro-sumer run-and-gun camera – so-called because you can run with it while gunning for shots, leaving functions such as focus on automatic. It lacked the full range of professional features, but it had been all I could afford at the time and I'd taken a quiet pride in getting the shots I did with the equipment I had.

For *Blencathra* I upgraded my simple run-and-gun to a camera that was small and

The *Scafell* showing on BBC4 was a game-changer. Suddenly I was earning decent royalties – money that until now I'd only dreamt about.

▶ **Morning mists, St John's in the Vale.**

▲
The distinct knuckled ridges of Blencathra from the air.

◀
Sunset in Newlands Valley.

The film would be shot differently, edited differently, and while it might feel like a continuation of *Scafell*, stylistic changes would set it apart.

light enough to fit in my pack so I didn't need to lug it around on my shoulder. I used that on 'people shoots', as I call them, when out and about on the fell, walking and talking. I also invested in a Sony Alpha 7S – a mirrorless DSLR with full-frame sensor. While also small and light, its autofocus was not as good as that of the run-and-gun, so I used it mainly for fellscape scenes where I prefer manual focus.

Finally, I bought a 6D DSLR, which was Canon's cheapest full-frame model at the time. I didn't always carry all of the cameras; I took what was appropriate for each shoot. I also upgraded my microphones to improve sound quality. I've used the same kit on *Helvellyn* – even the Canon 6D, which is now battered and covered in tape.

Getting to grips with my new kit had to happen fast. I wanted the trilogy's second instalment to be complete within 14 months – a self-imposed deadline to maximise on the interest created by *Scafell*'s TV success, and because I wanted it to première in May, as *Scafell Pike* had done. I believed the tighter schedule was achievable, given Blencathra's accessibility compared to that of remote West Cumbria and the Scafells, and because my new equipment enabled me to edit on the go.

My walking on Blencathra had until now focussed on Hall's Fell Ridge and Sharp Edge, and I needed to consider how to portray the whole mountain through the seasons rather than just these obvious arêtes of high drama. At that point I hadn't a clue how I might bring all that about, and my unfamiliarity with how the weather and sunlight played on Blencathra – and the great morning sidelight that blazed east from Eden – meant a greater element of chance would come into play.

The film would be shot differently, edited differently, and while it might feel like a continuation of *Scafell*, stylistic changes would set it apart. For example, the interviews in *Scafell Pike* had mostly been conducted straight to camera, and often indoors. In *Blencathra*, more are conducted outdoors, and feature cutaways, where the sound of the interviewee's voice is accompanied by mountain footage.

The fellscape sequences were also treated differently, in part because of Blencathra's gentler aesthetic and terrain. *Scafell Pike*'s journey through the seasons was clearly defined, with introductory sequences for spring, summer, autumn, and winter, but in *Blencathra* those seasonal transitions are subtler, except for winter's, which has a dramatic introduction for no other reason than winter is my favourite time of year. I also injected a little more humour, with scenes such as Stuart Maconie, Ed Byrne and David Powell-Thompson on Sharp Edge. I tried to make the changes subtle, so as not to alienate those who liked *Scafell Pike*, and I could only hope that *Blencathra*'s audience would feel as engaged as they had been for its predecessor. If the approach worked, I would do things differently again when it came to *Helvellyn*: three distinct films that felt like one.

Home from home

Shortly after starting work on *Life of a Mountain: Blencathra*, I met Tim Foster, head of the Field Studies Council's Blencathra Centre, near Threlkeld.

Tim was generosity personified. Appreciating the struggles I would face over the coming months with accommodation and hauling my equipment around – not only on the fells, but also on the train between Newark and Penrith – he put the centre's facilities at my disposal. Whenever he was able, he offered me rooms in the centre's dorms and on-site cottages, as well as food, even though I could shop in nearby Keswick.

His wife, the artist Sue Foster, has a studio on site in which I was able to store my kit so that I could travel between Penrith and Newark with just a day pack. Meanwhile, the accessibility to Blencathra offered by the centre meant I didn't have to camp as much as I had on Scafell Pike. Living beneath the mountain, I could head out pre-dawn, capture footage, return to the centre, then strike out again for sunset. When I did camp it was for the sheer joy of wild camping and to maintain that connection with the landscape that only an overnight stay can bring.

The people's mountain

Life of a Mountain: Blencathra is bookended by David Powell-Thompson, opening and closing the film just as shepherdess Alison O'Neill had done in *Scafell Pike*.

Knowing each other so well made for an easy shoot. We camped out together on Threlkeld Knotts below Clough Head the night before filming the opening scenes, for which David spoke to the camera unscripted. I had given him a number of bullet points of things I wanted him to address, and he'd jotted his own ideas down too, but when he spoke on camera the words flowed naturally. The only scripted line was his declaration in the closing scene that Blencathra was "the people's mountain".

"Whatever else we talk about, it has got to finish with that line," I told him. The phrase reflects not only the fact that it's such a well-loved fell, but was also a wink and a nod to the movement that had grown to buy the fell for the nation. By the time the film was finished I had the distinct feeling – from my dealings with the estate and conversations with locals – that the sale was not going to proceed; and indeed, having found other ways to settle his tax bill, the Earl took the mountain off the market in June 2016. Nevertheless, the phrase reinforced the message that every fell – not just Blencathra – is ultimately a people's mountain.

When I did camp it was for the sheer joy of wild camping and to maintain that connection with the landscape that only an overnight stay can bring.

▶ **Aurora above wild camp on Bannerdale Crags.**

▲
David Powell-Thompson on Esk Pike looking into Great Langdale.

▲ **David Powell-Thompson battling the snows on Gategill Fell looking west to Skiddaw.**

We decided to film the closing sequence in winter, and set off from the field centre for Blease Fell during a storm that had brought a dump of snow to the tops. We were trailblazing, ploughing a fresh trail towards the summit, but the soft, unconsolidated snow made it harder and harder to discern contours, let alone the route. Normally, even fully laden with kit, I'd be on Blease Fell in an hour, but today the constant holing-up slowed us down and the ascent took two-and-a-half hours. As we approached the summit, strong winds forced us to crawl over the snow.

"I'm an old man, you know!" David complained, over the gusts.

"Age is a state of mind, David."

"Eff off!"

I had entertained ideas about filming David on the summit at sunset, but conditions were too bad to film and, knowing his availability for filming was restricted, I had to settle for footage of him wandering the summit.

I'd had enough of walking in the snow and couldn't wait to get back down for a pint. Sat on my pack, I slid most of the way down into the valley, where conditions were mild and sunny; those 2,000 feet made a hell of a difference.

When we came to film the closing scenes two weeks later we returned instead to the more peaceful viewpoint of Threlkeld Knotts where we'd filmed the opener. The more I thought about it, the more the location made sense. David was back where he'd started, but in a different season – the year had come full circle.

We were trailblazing, ploughing a fresh trail towards the top, but the soft, unconsolidated snow made it harder and harder to discern contours, let alone the route.

The dropping of the 't' was at the instigation of the Royal Mail, to avoid confusion over addresses, which is why we now have Wastwater and Wasdale.

Incredible histories
Before starting *Blencathra*, I found myself missing the Scafells, so I headed back west to make a walking DVD with David Powell-Thompson – *The Lake District: Upper Eskdale*.

Knocking *Upper Eskdale* out in four weeks was bloody hard work, but we shared some good times and learned much from each other. On one walk on Scafell Pike I was able to tell David about a ruined summit shelter there, perhaps 150 yards south of the summit, which had a fireplace once upon a time. I'd first come across it a decade earlier. By the time we revisited it the fireplace had collapsed, and people had used the shelter as a bin and a toilet, but we could still discern the structure. I think many people are oblivious to it because it blends in with the rocks and boulders. We discussed theories. Was it a Victorian tea hut? Could it have been built by the Ordnance Survey staff who camped up there for an entire summer in the 1800s waiting for perfect conditions in which to see Snowdon in Wales, the Merrick in Scotland, Ingleborough in Yorkshire and other hills? This was the survey that resulted in the 'w' being dropped from the name 'Scawfell' and saw 'Wastdale' become 'Wasdale'. The dropping of the 't' was at the instigation of the Royal Mail to avoid confusion over addresses, which is why we now have Wastwater and Wasdale.

▲ **Band of light, Blencathra.**

▶ **Winter storm over the Naddle valley.**

Another thing I learned from David was the existence of a little packhorse bridge over Countess Beck, where the back road from Gosforth meets the road from Nether Wasdale to Wasdale Head. Many people miss it because they're driving to the start of the walk up Scafell Pike. It's called Countess Bridge – it was built as a memorial to a countess – but the name means nothing to most people.

One of the strangest facts I learned, though, is about a patch of land that lies near Nether Wasdale, just off the Santon Bridge road as you're heading towards Wastwater. Cresting the hill near Irton Pike, there's such a fantastic view down towards Gable and the valley head that you have to stop the car and get out for a look.

The ground on the right there stands out because it doesn't look like surrounding farmland – instead it looks like it's been landscaped. And that's because it has.

There was going to be a golf club and hotel there but the project was scrapped at the outbreak of the First World War. The landscaping had already been done, and while it has weathered a bit over the last hundred years it still resembles a deer park. These are the kind of things David and I try to include in the DVDs so that they don't get forgotten. History is everywhere if you look for it in the landscape.

Thre'keld born and bred

As holiday properties become increasingly prevalent in Lakeland, so born and bred folk are becoming harder to find. I wanted to include someone in *Life of a Mountain: Blencathra* who had known the place for years and who could point out some of the changes that have taken place in recent decades. Plenty of people recommended Willy Tyson, who farmed at Middle Row. A real character, I was assured; there was nothing Willy didn't know about the area, or about sheep. He also liked a pint, they said – though I'm not sure why they thought that was a recommendation in my eyes!

Willy was not up for appearing on camera, but he recommended Donald Angus, Threlkeld born and bred and a respected member of the village community. I knocked on his door and was greeted by a down-to-earth, no-nonsense northern bloke. Donald's a smart guy – a parish councillor with a fascination for the area. He was perfect for the role I envisaged and more than happy to share his knowledge. He recalled where the village smithy and post office had been, what the pub had been like when it was a gathering place for the local hunt, and how Gategill Fell was once known locally as Dan Fell, after a local farmer. Blease Road, which leads to the field centre, was once called Old Sanny Road, or Duck Lane, he told me, because there were always ducks on it.

It was interesting to uncover these stories, which had otherwise been lost in time, and to learn things that even Alfred Wainwright – "Nobody liked Wainwright," Donald said – had not picked up on. Donald told me there never used to be a track along the top of Blencathra – what he called the "big grassy sward". A lot of these paths have only come into existence since Wainwright's guides became popular, but there are serious trails – and sometimes scars – on the ground today. I occasionally bump into Donald when I'm in the area and still enjoy a chat.

▲ **Steve on the summit ridge of Blencathra, backed by an atmospheric sunrise.**

◀ **North Pennines sunrise from Sheffield Pike.**

Steve Birkinshaw had run 320 miles over the 214 Wainwrights in an astonishing six days and 13 hours.

Running late

Early on September 11, 2015, I left the Field Studies Centre and scaled Blease Fell for a dawn meeting with fell runner Steve Birkinshaw. The summer before, to great acclaim, Steve had run 320 miles over the 214 Wainwrights in an astonishing six days and 13 hours, breaking the record Joss Naylor had held for 27 years.

Steve lived across the valley from Blencathra and, depending on the weather, could be found running up there most days. Including him in the film would continue the fell-running theme established by Joss in *Life of a Mountain: Scafell Pike*, so Steve and I met in the White Horse at Scales one evening to discuss the idea. More than a few pints later, we finished the evening a little the worse for wear having agreed to arrange dates for filming.

The first shoot was in Steve's front room, and the weather that day was too grim for the shots I really wanted of him out on Blencathra. A week later, therefore, we met just before dawn, high on the cold and windy summit of Blease Fell. It was late summer, so sunrise wasn't too early – about 6.30am – and light was starting to break as I finished setting up the camera. I asked Steve to run back and forth along the summit ridge time and again while I captured footage of him during an atmospheric sunrise.

As soon as I'd grabbed what I wanted, we enjoyed a brief chit-chat before he set off for work at Newcastle University, while I returned to the field centre, and breakfast.

To my mind, the best times to film are dawn and dusk – ideally when there's broken cloud in the sky and a clear horizon, so that when the sun comes up or drops it sets off the cloud.

At sunrise and sunset there's a lot going on in the sky, and an intensity of colour and contrast that lights the fells in dramatic fashion. When there's mist or fog in the valleys the drama is heightened further.

I don't usually film during the day, but in winter, when the sun is lower in the sky, you often get arresting side-light, with associated shadows and contrasts.

I hate summer. I don't like the heat, and to me the fells look dull and green. I restrict fellscape filming to dawn and dusk. The exception is during storms, when even during summer months you can capture worthwhile footage, and windy days, when driven, broken cloud is ideal for time lapses.

Autumn and winter are my favourite times of year because you've got more intense colours, low sun, mist in the valleys, frost and dustings of snow, all combined. What's more, I don't have to get out of bed early to capture the magic! That's why most of my wild camps occur in summer – because I have to stay out on the fell late in the evening to catch the sunset and be up with the lark at dawn. On these camps I rarely get any more than four hours' kip.

Autumn and winter are my favourite times of year because you've got more intense colours, low sun, mist in the valleys, frost and dustings of snow, all combined.

At the Sharp end

The sequence covering the late-summer ascent of Sharp Edge served two purposes. First, it demonstrated that the near-vertical hands-on route up the dramatic arête – one of the finest scrambles in Lakeland – should not be under-estimated. As I accompanied walkers with my run-and-gun camera, a drone would capture the action from above, emphasising the dramatic nature of the ridge and just how exposed those attempting the ascent are.

Second, it injected a dose of humour into the film. I envisaged the sequence as a *Last of the Summer Wine*-style scene: three chaps, each different in character, their personalities becoming apparent as they scrambled up the notorious arête onto Atkinson Pike.

There was cocky, confident Ed Byrne, who gave the impression that he was not frightened of anything. Beyond readership of *The Great Outdoors* magazine, for which he writes a regular column about his adventures, few people were aware that the Irish comedian has an interest in the outdoors. After he followed

▶ **A lone walker heads for Gategill Fell.**

me on Twitter I pinged him a private message to see if he was up for appearing in the scene. Having not done Sharp Edge before, he was intrigued by the idea.

Then there was Stuart Maconie, the figure to whom most of the audience could perhaps relate. He had also never tackled the ridge. It was Maconie who made the sequence. He was genuinely frightened by the scramble and swore afterwards that he would never do it again. His honesty and humility won the audience's empathy, rather like Peter Sallis's *Summer Wine* character Norman Clegg. Ironically, to my mind Maconie came across as funnier than Byrne in the film – the radio presenter out-funnying the funny guy.

Finally there was David Powell-Thompson, who knew the fell like the back of his hand, and who was there to guide Ed and Stuart and oversee safety. That way, anything that went wrong would be on his insurance, not mine! His role was also my nod-and-a-wink to a scene he'd appeared in during Julia Bradbury's *Wainwright Walks* TV series, when he guided her along the same ridge; like Maconie, Julia had been frightened.

David came across as the wise old man of the trio and I hoped that the chemistry between them would shine through, making the sequence both entertaining and subliminally informative, emphasising the care necessary even on something as short and sweet as Sharp Edge. The scene was all one-take stuff – as authentic as it could be.

Before we set off from Scales Tarn I explained that I wanted them to make some reference to the fact that Sharp Edge is a blackspot for mountain rescue, and to mention its old name, Razor's Edge.

"The rest," I told them, "is up to you."

The day took a lot of planning and I had to be fully on the ball. Both Willy Tyson, who then farmed by Blencathra, and the Earl of Lonsdale's estate had granted permission for a quad bike and trailer to convey the commercial Flying Glass drone team to the summit. Lonsdale Settled Estates does not own all of Blencathra but it does have a big chunk – the exciting bit, basically: the front face, and half of Sharp Edge. The arête marks its boundary. Some people claim to have experienced problems dealing with Lonsdale Settled Estates, but I had no issues. Whenever I sought permission to film on its land, it was given.

The drone team members were fans of the Scafell movie and had volunteered their services and the use of their professional drone – including a £30,000 camera – in return for a credit in the film. They were very experienced,

▲ **Stuart Maconie and Ed Byrne on Sharp Edge.**

I envisaged the sequence as a *Last of the Summer Wine*-style scene: three chaps, each different in character, their personalities becoming apparent as they scrambled up Sharp Edge.

▲
Sharp Edge from the air.

but even so, I was specific about where and how I wanted them to capture the action. I set out grid references I wanted them to adhere to, laid down times at which the film needed to roll, and was pernickety about how they went about it: "Why are you panning the camera like I would down on the fell?," I would ask. "You need to be moving within the scene to emphasise the fact that it's in the air." And: "This is the composition I want; this is the light I want you to capture – this is the colour I'm after." Drama was what I wanted. They could give the static, sunny, daytime scenes to *Countryfile*!

In the end, however, the carefully laid plans came to nothing; it was too windy for the drone to take off, which meant all of the day's footage had to come from the run-and-gun camera.

I was moving to and fro along the ridge, filming David, Ed and Stuart from behind and ahead in strong winds, constantly stopping and starting. Filming with them was easy, despite the challenges of working against the wind, as they were already comfortable in front of a camera. I didn't have to direct them over which direction they needed to be looking – they were in tune with where I was pointing the camera and when I was recording. They knew when to finish and pause, and they understood why I needed them to keep traversing the Edge – so I could gather shots from different angles.

Occasionally we would have to take a breather because Maconie was, to put it politely, bricking it. The fact that I was wearing trekking sandals mortified him. We paused occasionally to let other scramblers pass by, or when the wind was gusting too strongly. Those quiet moments, when the three could relax, were when I was able to record some of their banter while they were unaware I was filming. Some wonderfully authentic material came from those moments.

My friend Dan Richards, son of guidebook author Mark, was helping out on the day, carrying a pack containing some of my equipment and our lunches. That enabled me to move along the ridge more safely, unencumbered. He also acted as a spotter, standing behind me to ensure I didn't accidentally step backwards and fall to my death while engrossed in filming. At one point I was swapping a camera from the pack when a gust caught the pack; thankfully we didn't instinctively try to grab it – we just watched as it tumbled down the rock face. Luckily I'd got the camera out before it went.

Occasionally we would have to take a breather because Maconie was, to put it politely, bricking it.

From above, the pack – a robust model – looked undamaged, but when Dan retrieved it after the shoot we found it had been ripped to shreds: our pies and sandwiches wrecked. The accident demonstrated the results of a 100-foot fall down Sharp Edge. What if the pack had been flesh and bone? It didn't bear thinking about.

A painful edit

Quite a few things had gone wrong that day, what with the pack taking a tumble, the lack of drone and the buffeting wind. I was pleased, though, with how the sequence came out: it was funny, and the message came across loud and clear: the arête is an environment in which you need to take considerable care. It sells the dangers of Sharp Edge.

There was one problem on the day, however, that I didn't share with the others. I'd been aware of it from the outset, but worried that admitting it might make me look unprofessional. Due to a fault with my camera's microphone settings, the entire day was shot without sound. David, Maconie and Byrne were wired up with individual tie-clip mics, as I knew the camera's on-board microphone would not have picked up their voices over a distance; nevertheless, the sound on the camera was essential for syncing audio and video during editing.

Tie-clip mics ensure you can always hear a person's voice. Unlike sound captured by the camera's mic, tie-clip mic recordings tend to be clear, though you have less control over audio levels: the audio might peak and distort; the wind can hit the mic and ruin a recording; and the mic can be inadvertently knocked when a jacket's done up or when a collar rubs against it.

The day after the shoot I reviewed everything on my laptop, and was relieved to find that the tie-clip mics had done their job perfectly: the audio was good and the shoot was not entirely lost. When it came to syncing the footage with the sound recordings, however, I had to lip-read instead of simply matching the different audio tracks. In all, the process took a pain-staking two weeks; an important lesson learned.

Another factor I need to consider when mixing audio is ambient sound. Tie-clip mic audio sounds like it has been recorded in a sterile studio and has none of the feel of being on the fell – no noise of wind in the heather, of sheep, becks or birdsong – so I mix the mic'ed signal with ambient sound from another field microphone so that you hear the clarity of the voice alongside an organic backdrop. Sometimes I might leave a camera by a wall

◀
Morning mists from the Blencathra Centre.

I don't want to be carrying bulky, heavy equipment all over the fells when kit that is smaller and lighter still gives professional quality. It's not a matter of having the best kit – it's how to best use what you've got.

▼
Wild camping.

to capture the sound of the breeze to use as ambient sound. On other days, when I'm filming the fells and I don't want to take a microphone, I use ambient audio captured a day or week before.

I've picked up a few tips on recording audio from the internet, but as you shoot more you learn what works. Better sound quality typically means investing more in equipment, though the microphones I use are very affordable. There are little tricks that help eke the most out of my kit. So while I might not use the most expensive cameras or microphones, there are ways and means of making the film sound and look like it was done on equipment five or ten times the price. I'm not just saying that because I've got Yorkshire blood in me: it's because I don't want to be carrying bulky equipment over the fells when kit that is smaller and lighter still gives professional quality. A lot of the time it's not a matter of having the best kit – it's knowing how to best use what you've got.

Sunday lunch paranoia

It first happened after *Scafell* had been on television: a gentleman came over to me in a bar and declared: "You're that Abraham fella. My family have been coming to Wasdale Show every year and they always stay in The Strands Inn – now they can't get a bloody room!"

I'm always surprised to be recognised by people when out and about. How do they know who I am? After all, I'm behind the camera – never in front of it. Yet I've been stopped not just around the Lake District and Newark, but in Manchester, Aviemore, Glasgow, London – even Kathmandu. "Hey, you're that guy! You made the Scafell film!"

Although over time I've grown used to it, being recognised is something I never anticipated, and initially I found it unsettling. On one occasion I was having a post-walk pint in the White Horse at Scales. I'd been there about half an hour, reading one of Wainwright's guides, when I noticed people staring at me and started to feel paranoid. I texted Sue and asked her to arrive sooner rather than later; I wanted to get dinner over and head somewhere else. Just before she turned up, however, the people came over and started to chat. I hadn't been paranoid – they *had* been staring because they recognised me, but they just wanted to talk about my work. Paranoid no more, I could enjoy my Sunday lunch.

On other occasions, when I've been out filming, people have wandered in front of the camera and asked: "Are you filming? Are you Terry Abraham?"

Well, yeah, I *was* filming until you walked into shot!

I don't really mind the attention, but I'm a private person at heart. It's nice that I'm recognised for my films, but I'd rather my films did the talking. And if I'm in the pub I tend to want to wind down and collect my thoughts after being out on the fell.

Stuart Maconie advised me to learn to deal with attention, though there would be times, he said, when it can get awkward – when you're about to have Sunday dinner and your meal is getting cold, for example, or even in the gents.

Storm Desmond hits

On December 5, 2015, at the height of the tempest, Blencathra Field Centre director Tim Foster and I scaled Latrigg to witness the effects of Storm Desmond. The storm had already dumped a record amount of rain on the area, the weather station on Honister Pass having recorded 341mm – more than 13 inches – within 24 hours. The flooding had devastated communities around Cumbria and beyond. Particularly badly hit were villages such as Staveley, Glenridding and Pooley Bridge.

So much rain had fallen that the River Derwent had burst its banks and the lakes of

The flooding had devastated communities around Cumbria and beyond. Particularly badly hit were villages such as Staveley, Glenridding and Pooley Bridge.

▲
Camp on Souther Fell: where Terry decided to film *Blencathra*.

Derwent Water and Bassenthwaite had become one. Some scientists believe that the two lakes had been a single water body thousands of years ago, and it was the recurrence of that which Tim and I had planned to witness. As it was, the cloud was too thick, and the weather too bad; we were forced off the fell.

We headed into Keswick, and as we got to Fitz Park we noticed TV crews among the crowds of onlookers and realised that things were not at all good. I bumped into a couple of mates from Keswick Mountain Rescue Team who asked if I was there to film the storm's effects. I explained that Tim and I were simply passing through.

"You need to get out of Keswick now," came the reply. "There's only going to be one way in and out of town soon." Council staff were closing off the bridges in anticipation of static caravans washing downstream and taking the bridges out. Alarms were sounding, people were being told to leave town... We jumped into the 4x4 and escaped back to the field centre.

The following day visibility improved as the cloud lifted from the fells to reveal the carnage. I was receiving requests from news agencies and messages from journalists asking whether I was safe, if I still had internet access and, if so, could I upload photographs and footage for them. I declined them all. I didn't want to film the misery of local people. "Come and see it for yourself," I told them. "What I'm seeing is not good; I know a lot of folk in this area and they're ruined."

At first I didn't consider shooting flood footage for *Life of a Mountain* because it felt voyeuristic. I also wanted my film to have a timeless feel, like that of its predecessor; covering such an event risked dating it. I'd felt the same way about covering the campaign to buy Blencathra, which was already underway when I'd started shooting the film.

As I toured the area in the wake of Storm Desmond, I was heartbroken by the impacts

▲
In calmer times: the classic view of Catbells over Derwent Water from Friar's Crag.

on families and livelihoods. For the first time in memory, Keswick had become a ghost town. While it was novel to encounter only locals, it brought home to me just how few people actually live in Keswick – the town is overwhelmed with holiday lets and second homes, and after the disaster the majority had stayed away.

Locals began to ask when I would be recording the devastation. Initially I couldn't understand why they were asking the question, but more and more people insisted that I needed to capture what they were describing as a historic moment. One person implored me not to let "those effing southerners" forget about the plight of affected Cumbrians once the floods had fallen off the news headlines. "There's long-term harm in this," he warned.

Reluctantly, therefore, I started thinking about how I might record the aftermaths of the storm. It didn't matter that I'd already missed the worst of the deluge, as I didn't want to cover the storm in the general way the news media had. Instead of filming flooded streets and buildings I wanted to focus on the intimacy of the human side of the story. That, I hoped, might make the message behind the tragedy more enduring. Agriculture, I reasoned, is a major part of the area's identity, but all the media focus so far had been on towns and villages – not individuals living in rural isolation. Questions about what was being done for those in such situations needed to be asked.

At Low Bridge End Farm in St John's in the Vale, farmer Sarah Chaplin-Brice, her husband, Graham and their family had borne the brunt of Desmond's damage. Access to their farm was across one of several bridges in the area that had been washed away. As well as running the farm, the family had been involved with outdoor education in their fellside woodlands. Before the storm struck, Graham and other locals had been monitoring the water table

Instead of filming flooded streets and buildings I wanted to focus on the intimacy of the human side of the story.

at Thirlmere and had warned United Utilities that water needed to be let out of the reservoir before the rains arrived. But no one could have foreseen just how much rainfall would come. I had thought it might even turn to snow, but the jet stream shifted and the cold air didn't hit, so all the moisture fell as rain instead. Sarah and son Will were among those telling me that I needed to film the devastation caused by the storm. Their message was: "Don't let the rest of the country forget us."

I was reluctant to intrude, but they couldn't have been more welcoming. Before the flood I'd filmed scenes of Will feeding his rare-breed sheep while Sarah described the work they did and their ventures into diversification, with accommodation and outdoor education. After Storm Desmond, I filmed her walking around the farm inspecting the destruction of bridges, riverbanks and their access track, and talking with National Park officials about what repairs might be possible. Filming the devastation at Low Bridge End was tough. You can see in the film, from the look on Sarah's face, that she was trying to be positive in the toughest of times: to me it's the film's most moving sequence.

In the end, perhaps the post-Desmond footage did date the film, but I'm glad I included it. My vision may originally have been to give *Blencathra* a timeless, classic feel, but as people have said since, each film is also a time capsule – a reflection of the highs and lows of life as it was in the valleys and on the felltops during the short period in which I was filming.

The mountain's voice

The Lake District has long inspired poets, writers and composers – not to mention a few film makers. Cumbria – and the north of England in general – is blessed with so many talented creative people who rarely receive the recognition they deserve, for no other reason than because they are not based in media-centric London. In *Scafell Pike* I'd hoped to add tributes to the fell in song, poem and performance, but was thwarted by time pressures and limited resources. With *Blencathra* I had an opportunity to put that right – to use the film as a platform to help raise the profile of creative folk; both locals and those drawn to the area by its beauty.

I will readily admit that poetry's not my thing, but I was eager to include a commissioned poem that captured the soul of Blencathra and the communities that surround it. Not knowing where to start, I posted on social media that I was seeking a poet. I received several responses and asked each to send examples of their work. It was important that their words moved me, but equally important, to my ears, was the poet's voice; I wanted the chosen poet to recite their poem on film, so the voice needed to carry authority and charisma.

Phil Houghton ticked all the boxes. Through his poem, 'Blencathra', he gave the film a link between Lakeland's contemporary writers and the Romantic poets of the late 18th and early 19th centuries, demonstrating how writers continue to be inspired to this day. His sequence – Phil walking his Border terrier Hamish – was nailed in a single shoot, with Blencathra the backdrop for his reading of 'Blencathra' the poem. The voice-over was recorded in his car immediately after filming.

A second creative voice came to the film through a shared love of the outdoors.

Since *Scafell Pike*, a number of musicians had been in touch looking to get involved in my work, but songwriter Lee Maddison contacted me seeking advice about wild camping. It was only as we chatted about tents and backpacking kit that I realised I was talking to a songwriter and musician. Later, I listened to a few of his songs and enjoyed one in particular – 'Where Eagles Fly' – and saw an opportunity for the film.

Lee usually performs with a collective of musicians under the name Maddison's Thread, based in the north east. However, having heard something in the song I believed could be accentuated, I wanted him to treat 'Where Eagles Fly' differently. First, I asked him to rewrite the lyrics to speak about Blencathra. I then explained I wanted a different arrangement of the song: "If you have access to a studio, I want just you, your voice and the guitar, and perhaps the backing vocals. Nothing more." I then sent his new stripped-down recording to my soundtrack composer Freddie to work his magic on.

I remember playing the acoustic version – just Lee and his guitar – to friends, who seemed underwhelmed. I told them: "You're not hearing what I'm hearing. Once Freddie gets in there with a brass section and strings, and the music is accompanied by footage of dawn and dusk, you'll love it."

And that's exactly what happened. When Freddie emailed the finished version of the song, now renamed 'The Mountain', I felt a lump in my throat. And when the naysayers saw the finished clip, they were sold. That song – effectively a self-contained music video within the film – is a tribute to the mountain in song. The melody and lyrics are Lee's, the arrangement is Freddie's, and it is one of my favourite parts of the film.

"Once Freddie gets in there with a brass section and strings, and the music is accompanied by footage of dawn and dusk, you'll love it."

The film's third creative aspect – a community choir singing about a connection with the landscape – was another idea that I'd not had a chance to realise for *Scafell Pike* but put right in *Blencathra*. Cockermouth-based choir Sing Owt, which focusses on songs about the area, seemed perfect for the role and director Dave Camlin was keen to give my ideas a go. While the melody and lyrics for the song 'The Mountain' had been Lee Maddison's, arranged by Freddie, in this instance I asked Dave to put lyrics to the main theme Freddie had composed for the film. Dave also created an arrangement for a public performance of the song, which I planned to film. It occurred to me that some might regard the inclusion of both Lee's song and the choir's performance as overkill, but, I thought: "It's my film, I like 'em both. They're staying."

Sing Owt usually performs outdoors, where the massed voices resemble the sound of a Welsh male-voice choir, but the recording took place when the area was still being battered by the tail-end of Storm Desmond, so instead

▲ **Home from home: the Blencathra Centre (top), and clouds over Skiddaw House (below).**

▶ **Heat haze in the Northwestern Fells.**

▲
Autumnal front over
Bleaberry Fell.

▲
Sing Owt, singing out.

> I regard the spoken-word and musical tributes to *Blencathra*, together with the Sharp Edge 'Summer Wine' sequence and a handful of others, as the beating heart of the film.

the choir and a small audience gathered in Threlkeld Village Hall.

I was working solo for the shoot, with only my run-and-gun camera. We did three takes: one for wide-angle group shots; a second in which I got a little closer; and then a third when I moved among the group catching facial expressions.

I regard the spoken-word and musical tributes to *Blencathra*, together with the Sharp Edge *Summer Wine* sequence, and perhaps a handful of others such as the introduction of the winter chapter, as the beating heart of the film. They are the embodiment of my love for the fell.

Sharp Edge in winter

Conditions were perfect when I filmed a mountaineer's gallivanting winter ascent of the frozen Sharp Edge. The snow was good, deep and consolidated, and there was barely a breeze. I had tackled Sharp Edge on many occasions before, and knew it well, but I'd never traversed it in winter conditions. Dan Richards – credited as 'Sherpa' in the closing titles – was on hand to assist again, minding equipment and acting as spotter for my drone from an often-overlooked flat area at the foot of the ridge which, on another occasion, might offer a nice place to camp.

We did ground-level shots and the mountaineer's comments to camera first, and I set a camera on a tripod to film from afar, while navigating the drone. Dan's role as spotter fulfilled a legal requirement to maintain eye contact with the device at all times. While Dan monitored the drone's position, I was able to check the footage it was capturing. Drones are not easy to control at the best of times, and anticipating gusts coming over the ridge and through the cols made it doubly difficult.

Before heading for the foot of the arête, we discussed where I wanted the mountaineer to pause during our ascent, and what I wanted him to do during those pauses. The mountaineer practically danced up the arête, yapping away to himself throughout. He and I both knew the route well: we knew where to stop and where we could pass each other as I skipped back and forth to gain different shots. He was relaxed, though constantly mindful of the potential dangers: that sense of self-preservation is the reason he has always come back alive from his expeditions on the world's great ranges.

While regarding myself first and foremost as a backpacker, I was well within my comfort zone on the shoot. I was wrapped up snug and wearing wellies – deer stalking wellies, designed for the fells – with crampons which gripped well to the ice. In fact, the perfectly frozen conditions offered perhaps the easiest walk I've done over Sharp Edge; I felt as though I could run across it. At no stage was I frightened – cautious maybe, nervous at times, but it's good to be that way: it's what keeps you alive. Things go wrong when you get cocky, and the same principle applies to filming: when I'm over-confident I'm far more likely to end up with disappointing results.

There are some routes in the Lake District I wouldn't attempt in winter, no matter how good the conditions. Jack's Rake on Pavey Ark is one; I regard it as more dangerous than Sharp Edge. People get a false sense of security from the fact they're ascending a gully, but the route involves tricky manoeuvres where accidents happen, no matter what the weather.

The Sharp Edge winter shoot was wrapped up in a single ascent. From the Atkinson Pike summit on Blencathra we made our way towards Bannerdale Crags, then headed back into the valley to meet a frozen Dan.

Moving to Cumbria

Towards the end of production on *Blencathra* a weather window appeared during which it seemed certain we would get a lot of snow. I

◀
Pre-dawn from Blease Fell looking to Keswick.

wanted footage of certain people out in winter conditions – David Powell-Thompson on the summit, snowboarders Marcus Fellow and Daniel Wilson, fell-walkers Darrell Grundy and Tom Jacobs – and had planned a number of shoots. Thankfully, all of the people I'd lined up managed to re-jig their diaries.

I pretty much timed the start perfectly: I'd said the first snows would arrive on the Tuesday or Wednesday, and that by the weekend there would be a good dump, and I was right. The weather changed over that period, however, and in the end I had just nine days of decent snow in which to film with my subjects, as well as shooting snowy fellscapes.

It kicked off a period of intense work that was both mentally and physically exhausting. For the next week-and-a-bit I rose at four in the morning and returned to the Field Studies Centre after nine each night, getting food, necking a half bottle of wine and grabbing three or four hours' sleep before heading out to do it all over again. Friends became concerned at my appearance; they could see I was struggling.

"Don't worry, it's just another few days," I kept saying. "I'll do it. This weather won't be coming back – it may be my last chance to grab these winter shots."

On the penultimate night of the winter shoots I was sitting on the doorstep of my little cottage at the Blencathra Centre with a glass of port in the dark, and called Sue as snow began to fall again. As we chatted she started to cry. By then I'd been away from Newark for weeks and she was missing me. Physically exhausted and a little tipsy, I found myself shedding a few tears of my own.

"I don't want to go through this again. No more," she said. "Now the kids have flown, we're moving to Cumbria."

Moving to Cumbria!

I should have been ecstatic. For years Cumbria had felt like home – where I belonged

> My requirements for a new place to live were not demanding – I wanted a mobile phone signal and a pub nearby.

– and now Sue was proposing to make my long-held dream come true. Instead, sitting outside the field centre in the dark, with big white flakes falling, I felt overwhelmed. It would be a major life change, with lots to consider.

Sue, however, had worked it all out: we would get the house on the market and sold by January then make the move.

Give me a goal and I'll make it happen. So this time around, when filming was done I returned to Newark and gave our house a top-to-bottom makeover. Within weeks it looked like a show home and it sold in a fortnight. My requirements for a new place to live were not demanding – I wanted a mobile phone signal and a pub nearby – and in early January we relocated to Cumbria.

Even on the day we moved, I couldn't believe it was happening. A snowstorm was forecast and I'd told the removal men to be there in good time to avoid being trapped on the wrong side of the Pennines. Sure enough, the snow started falling when we arrived, and the removal guys had to spend the night in Penrith.

Our new home, an old cottage, was freezing that first night. The ancient Rayburn was struggling, and the doors had been open all day while we brought everything in. But a few hours later it was cosy and full of character; my little bit of heaven.

I've been welcomed with open arms. When friends and neighbours joke that I'm now a Cumbrian, I reply that I can never be that. "You're an honorary one," they say, by way of consolation.

I'll take that. I believe my neighbours can see how much I care about the area. They don't regard me as a patronising offcomer, lecturing them on what should and shouldn't be happening. I tend to fall on their side of most issues, and now that I've settled, I've become involved with local charities, and raising money for them.

Since moving up, I feel as though I've won the lottery and retired. I'm doing something I enjoy all the time, without the stress and hassle of travelling between Cumbria and Newark. I awake to the sights I love – the wildlife, the peace, the quiet, the fresh air, the cosy pubs... all of it. Finally my home is where my heart is.

None too shabby

Blencathra premièred at Rheged on May 14, 2016. I've often joked that it was my *Empire Strikes Back* to *Scafell*'s *Star Wars*. Many people prefer *Star Wars* to *The Empire Strikes Back*, and the Scafells film will always have a special place in my heart.

Blencathra was harder to film, aesthetically, and is better in technical terms, but given the time again, there are many things I would do differently – not just in terms of shooting fellscapes, but also involving more people who live in the area.

Even so, it turned out none too shabby a documentary that was another learning curve.

But as I watched the closing credits on the big Rheged screen my mind was already elsewhere: on the grand ridges and sheltered slopes that would backdrop the final film in my trilogy.

I awake to the sights I love – the wildlife, the peace, the quiet, the fresh air, the cosy pubs... all of it. Finally my home is where my heart is.

▲
Autumn mists over Gowbarrow Hall Farm.

PART FOUR

HELVELLYN

I WAS SAT BY THE FIRE WHEN I SUDDENLY FELT AN URGE TO WALK OUT OF THE DOOR, CLIMB CROSS FELL IN THE SNOWY DARK AND NEVER COME BACK.

A walk in the dark

Over the past decade, *Life of a Mountain* has dominated my life for long periods. After *Blencathra* I chose to take a ten-month break, partly to work on other projects, but mostly to recover from the intensity of production.

My recuperation, however, was to meet an abrupt end.

I'd been out mountain biking, exploring farmers' tracks and little-used bridleways in the Eden Valley. As night fell I made my way out of Bolton and was speeding down towards the River Eden when a bank of fog appeared. I know the road – it's got a couple of hairpins before you reach the bridge – and I'd started to slow, but the fog suddenly diffused the light from my bike lamps, virtually blinding me. "Bugger, that's not good," I thought, as I braked hard, then hit the verge, then flew like an arrow into the roadside dry-stone wall. Because I'd only popped out for a short ride, I'm ashamed to admit I wasn't wearing a helmet.

My memory of coming off the bike –and the rock wall shining white in the beam of my head torch as I flew towards it – is vivid. I remember the moment of impact – a shockwave through my head, into my neck and down the rest of my body; I remember a deafening crack in my eardrums; and I remember thinking: "This is it; I'm a gonner." When I came to I was lying face-down on the ground, mouth full of leaves and verge-dirt.

The first thing I did was try to move my toes – I was certain I'd broken my neck – and I felt them wriggle. I lifted my calves, bent my knees, shifted my fingers; I hadn't done any major damage to my back. I rolled over carefully and tilted my head up slightly; that felt OK too, other than an unfamiliar grinding noise.

I stood up slowly. The bike was smashed against the wall. I picked my head torch off the ground and lit my face to take a selfie and examine the damage. I thought I must've cracked my head open, but bar the dirt and a couple of grazes my face looked OK. "I'm a lucky guy," I thought.

A few seconds later I felt a warm sensation moving down my scalp, then blood started pouring down my face. I rang Sue immediately: she was seven minutes away while an ambulance was ten or 15. I was worried I might collapse by the road, I told her.

My memories of what happened next have faded. Sue tells me she insisted I rang Dan Richards. "Why?" I asked her, repeatedly, "He's too far away to help." But she wasn't expecting that; she wanted someone to keep me talking so I didn't lose consciousness.

When Sue arrived she chucked my trashed bike into the car, hung up on Dan and got me to hospital in Penrith. I was

◄ **Catstycam, with Helvellyn beyond.**

One afternoon we went up Hallin Fell and I was snapping away with the camera, gazing across Ullswater to Helvellyn, when I realised I'd been away for too long; it was time to start on my third and final film.

▼
Hallin Fell above Howtown from Arthur's Pike.

rushed straight in, at which point my memory fades again. I was kept in overnight, Sue a constant at my bedside.

Sue only told me afterwards that the doctors had said things were touch and go; not only were my injuries serious, but I was also in a state of extreme shock.

The Penrith nurses stitched me back together, cleaning dirt from the wounds that covered my face and scalp. When they were done I was left with one gash on my head and another below my eye. Sue took photos to show what a mess the accident had made of me, and what an idiot I'd been for not wearing a helmet. I was allowed home with a warning that I was likely to have severe concussion.

It was the first time I'd experienced concussion. You know when you walk into a room and think: "What did I come in here for?" I got that constantly. Not only was I confused; I also hated being stuck at home. I felt like a caged animal, desperate to get out. But my memory was shattered. I remembered almost nothing from the month before the accident and had to rely on others to tell me what I'd been up to.

As my days of healing became weeks, I fell into a deep depression. It wasn't a constant presence; instead it visited on certain days. It peaked one winter's evening when Sue was away with work down south and I was home alone. I was sat by the fire when I suddenly felt an urge to walk out of the door, climb Cross Fell in the snowy dark and never come back.

It was no idle thought; I got as far as the front door, but my cat – 'my little girl', I call her – wouldn't leave me alone. She kept miaowing and looking up at me, as though she knew something was wrong. I began crying like a baby, talking to my little girl, to the house... to myself, repeating the same words: "I don't know why, I don't know why..."

In time I snapped out of it and pinged Sue

a message. She rang back within a minute and insisted I make an appointment with the doctor. When I saw him he offered me happy pills, which I declined, despite his warning that depressive episodes could continue for six months or more. "You need to be active," I was told. "Get those happy hormones going by spending time outdoors." Because of my injuries and the problem with my memory, no-one except the doctor wanted me to go out. But sod them, I did.

Dan Richards was a tower of strength during those days. He would come to the house and take me on the fell in the snow, looking at red squirrels, spotting birds of prey. One afternoon we went up Hallin Fell and I was snapping away with the camera, gazing across Ullswater to Helvellyn, when I realised I'd been away for too long; it was time to start on my third and final film.

The urge came on suddenly, and it felt uncanny, because it was an earlier health scare that had kicked my arse into gear before *Scafell Pike*. Even so, it took a while to get back into the flow, and for a long time it was obvious I'd not recovered.

Some months later I was in the Dockray Hall pub in Penrith when the bar lady, Sandra, came over to me: "So you're back, then?" Her words took me by surprise. "The sparkle's back in your eyes," she continued.

I asked what she meant. "You were a nightmare, Terry," she replied. "Constantly asking the same things over and over. We'd tell you something and then two minutes later you were asking it again. I could see in your eyes that you weren't there. Now you're back. I can see it."

All the time in the world

In making *Helvellyn*, as with *Scafell*, I haven't let anyone rush me. I've done what I wanted to do, how and when I wanted to do it. *Blencathra*, produced in just 14 months, was too hurried; I could not – and would not – fit *Helvellyn* into a similar time frame.

When the queues on Striding Edge have gone home and the air is still, you can hear a pin drop from my perch on Lad Crag.

▲ **Wild camp on Lad Crag.**

Part of that was down to my slowly recovering health: I didn't want to risk burnout.

But mostly I wanted to nail a range of new, ambitious ideas – big sequences, smaller, more intimate scenes, and concepts I'd not been able to pin down in the past. Shooting would require a full two years.

A project of that scale could easily have become a disjointed mess, but I've put a lot of graft into *Helvellyn* and – unlike with its predecessors – have planned every detail. There's purpose to every scene and a link to the scene that follows; nothing is thrown in for the sake of it and everything is interwoven. A section on the future of farming leads into a discussion about conservation, which in turn leads into the area's cultural heritage, which leads into another subject...

Threaded into this narrative are a number of overarching messages. One of them is about the impact of our recreational activities on the landscape. Walking, cycling, climbing, kayaking, swimming... they may appear harmless, but they have consequences, affecting ecology, soil fertility, water quality and more.

Most of all I wanted *Helvellyn* to capture my love of wild places.

There's a crag – Lad Crag, just south of Helvellyn's summit – where I often camp. It's a quiet little spot, and you can get water from a nearby spring, Brownrigg Well, which flows all year round. Ravens reside on Lad Crag and the crags below into Nethermost Cove, and it's wonderful to sit by the cliff edge, at the porch of my tent, watching them swoop around, talking to each other, chasing, dancing in the air. Even on a summer's evening when it's still light at half-nine, there's no one else around. When the queues on Striding Edge have gone home and the air is still, you can hear a pin drop from my perch on Lad Crag.

When there's a job to do, your focus has to be on the camera. But when the footage has been captured, or when the camera's doing its thing during a time-lapse shoot, I can wander off and appreciate the moment. Just me, the breeze, those ravens... and the endless magic of the wild.

Chasing waterfalls

Ever since my cycling accident, Sue has kept a close eye on me. But she can't be with me all the time and in spring 2019, more than a year after the accident, I demonstrated that her caution was justified.

I was in the upper reaches of Aira Force, below Gowbarrow Fell above Ullswater. It was dawn and there was no-one else around. I was there to capture shots of the frozen waterfall using a GoPro fastened to a pole so that I could stick it underwater. I had my camera set up, the sun was breaking through the trees and I was enjoying the solitude when the next thing I knew I'd slipped and fallen 18 feet over rocks into the bowl of the waterfall.

I'll never forget being under the water and seeing my expensive iPhone – which I'd only just upgraded – trapped on a rock as the currents tried to wash it downstream. "I'm not losing that!" I thought, grabbing it, and jumping out of the water, hoping the phone was waterproof. At least the GoPro was. My clothes, however, were definitely not. I clambered onto the rocks in near-freezing conditions, soaked to the bone, stripped off and hung my clothes on branches in an effort to dry them.

It was only when my core temperature rose and I stopped shivering that I considered my situation: there I was, naked, above one of Lakeland's busiest tourist honeypots.

Thankfully I was in the quieter, higher reaches of the falls, and, by the time visitors appeared my clothes were almost dry. I quickly pulled on my torn jeans and jacket. But the shock was already sinking in. My arm was

It was only when my core temperature rose and I stopped shivering that I considered my situation: there I was, naked, above one of Lakeland's busiest tourist honeypots.

bruised and grazed, and the pain was agonising – even after necking paracetamol from my first aid kit. That afternoon my arm began to shake and I headed back to Penrith for a beer. Sue was livid. It was only then that she revealed how serious my cycling injuries had been a year earlier.

Flying high

The Lake District draws millions of visitors, many of whom come in search of the natural beauty, peace and quiet. Its high fells and narrow, twisting valleys also draw another kind of visitor: fighter pilots from air forces around the world who practise low-flying here to refine their skills. The noise and disturbance they cause may be the antithesis of Romantic Lakeland, but those jets make for a thrilling sight – one that draws its own breed of plane-spotting tourist.

Helvellyn features one of the most ambitious shoots I've tried my hand at to date: low-flying with the Royal Air Force through the Eastern Fells. The process of involving the RAF took more than a year, from first contact to filming with Air Commodore Nigel 'Wam' Wharmby who, coincidentally, lives below Helvellyn in Patterdale.

The jets fly out of RAF Leeming in North Yorkshire, and, on my first visit, shooting footage at the base, it was suggested I might like to go up in the plane myself.

I wasn't tempted. The footage would have to be captured on fixed cameras, which I'd be unable to adjust in-flight, so I would only have been going along for a free ride... And I don't much like flying.

Myself and University of Cumbria wildlife media student Nathan Buckley would therefore position ourselves at different locations on the ground to film the flight, while fixed GoPro cameras in Wam's aircraft – one facing forwards, one focussed on Wam's face – would capture the pilot's exhilarating view.

For the benefit of the forward-facing GoPro, the Hawk aircraft's canopy would be made spotlessly clean before take-off. We would trust to luck that the plane didn't strike any flies or run into rain, as streaks on the cockpit windscreen would ruin the images.

On the day of the flight I stationed myself near Aira Force, while Nathan was positioned above Brothers Water. I had a sweet shot set up to capture Wam curving around Place Fell with St Sunday Crag in the background. The jets were due to come through shortly, and I was primed to capture a sweeping shot as they sped past at around 400 knots (460 mph), when I had a sudden need to pee.

I looked at my watch.

I had two minutes until the jets were due.

There were other folk around so I dashed behind a tree and had just started to relieve myself when I heard the unmistakable sound of approaching aircraft. I ran back to the camera without tucking myself in and just managed to press record as they shot over the trees alongside Ullswater. We dubbed it the 'cock shot' – with apologies for the language.

In the end it wasn't quite the shot I'd wanted, and so, disappointed, we packed up and I

▶ **Autumnal Glenridding Dodd from Place Fell.**

▲
Helvellyn from the air whilst out with Matt Lindenberg.

headed to The Queen's Head in Askham. I was enjoying a cup of tea when my phone rang. It was Wam.

"We're off again in 50 minutes, mate."

"You're joking..."

I messaged Nathan to see if he could get back to Brothers Water sharpish. I thought I'd try to get back to Ullswater, but the road into Pooley Bridge was closed. Instead I hurried up Arthur's Pike. "No more mistakes," I thought, "or toilet breaks". The jets came through at almost the exact time Wam had said they would. They were difficult to film compositionally, partly because they moved so fast, and partly because they were so small against the backdrop of fells. In a wide-angle shot the jets were little more than dots, and I had to pan quickly – the closer they came, the faster I had to move the camera.

But this time around I did capture them, and Nathan messaged to say he'd done the same.

I took a moment to review the footage before packing up, and did a double take: the jets weren't Hawks, they were Typhoons. My heart sank; we'd filmed the wrong aircraft.

Then, just as I was coming to think the RAF shoot was jinxed – whoosh! – Wam flew over in his Hawk.

I couldn't believe it.

I messaged Nathan. "Don't worry, we've got footage. Don't delete it." I was sure we could work something out in the edit. I'd previously interviewed Wam in front of camera and he'd mentioned how Hawks sometimes chase Typhoons around the fells. That was enough to provide a narrative fix; no more shoots required.

For the film, I edited the order of the interview and manipulated the audio so that it sounds like Wam's voice is coming over the cockpit radio. In the cockpit footage you can't tell whether or not his mouth is moving as it's hidden under his oxygen mask – though you can just make out the moment when he breaks into a smile as he flies over Ullswater. In the raw footage you see Wam fly over Kirkstone Pass en route to Ullswater before passing Pooley Bridge. The flight lasts just 60 seconds.

Some of the high-altitude shots in the edit and elsewhere in the film I captured from my friend Matt Lindenberg's plane.

As we worked through sample shots I realised I needed something to protect the camera lens from reflections on the canopy. I considered draping a black cloth around my camera, secured to the glass with suckers, but I needed to be able to see all around as we were flying, so that was impractical.

Time for some egg timer-style DIY improvisation...

For drinking at camp I had a silicone cup with a hard rim to prevent it collapsing when full of liquid. I cut the rim off and replaced it with the kind of flexible draught-excluder seal used on doors and windows. That gave the cup rigidity, while allowing some give when pushed against the canopy, making a good seal. I then cut off the base so the cup fit snugly around the lens.

My DIY lens shield still wasn't perfect. A problem came to light after one of the test flights: the cup's blue interior was affecting the camera's white balance, giving the footage a blue tinge. So I painted it matt black. The end result was an enclosed camera effectively sealed to the canopy glass with no intrusive reflections.

I got a cheeky thrill imagining production companies seeing the shots and wondering how they were achieved without a £50,000 Cineflex camera. Here's the answer: it was my regular handheld video camera, a rubber cup and a tin of paint.

Moments of magic

August bank holiday 2019 brought something of a mini-heatwave. On the Sunday evening I checked the weather charts and clocked the possibility of a cloud inversion the following morning.. Inversions are not as common in

▲ **Air Commodore Nigel 'Wam' Wharmby leaves the hangar at RAF Leeming.**

I took a moment to review the footage before packing up, and did a double take: the jets weren't Hawks, they were Typhoons. My heart sank; we'd filmed the wrong aircraft.

summer as they are in autumn or winter and I put the odds at 50-50. Even if there was one, it would be unlikely to last long and would start lifting, I guessed, by half-eight and burn off by late morning.

It was last-minute, but I packed my bivvy and jumped on the bike. At Glenridding I started up Sheffield Pike, pouring with sweat. It was the first time I'd ridden my new electric bike up one of the bigger fells and I had to push the thing a lot of the way – you're not supposed to cycle on footpaths. I got up there at seven o'clock, dumped the bike, bivvied and relaxed. Back down in Glenridding there had been thousands of people, and on the path below White Stones I'd encountered hundreds more returning from Helvellyn. But branching off onto Sheffield Pike I had the place to myself, and I didn't see another soul until I returned to Glenridding next morning.

I captured some time-lapse footage: one of the shots I'd hoped to capture for the summer chapter was a night-time view down Ullswater towards Pooley Bridge, moon high above the cloud that was spilling across the lake and filling the valley. My attempt to capture footage of the stars wasn't as successful: the camera failed because of the cold, and the light of the moon, which was more than 50 per cent full, drowned out the stars (if you want to shoot stars, wait for a crescent moon).

But the dawn scenes… that's where it was at. Next morning, as predicted, there was a full cloud inversion. I was up at six, just before the sun kissed the felltops as it rose above the cloud sea in the valley. I enjoyed a good three or four hours of shooting, and left the camera rolling as I had my morning coffee, admiring the majesty of it all. As forecast, the cloud lifted at about eight o'clock, and I packed up and headed down, a happy man. Having been up so early, it felt like lunchtime when I reached Glenridding, ready for a pint.

Sometimes a shoot captures exactly what you had in your mind's eye. At other times the conditions deliver something unexpected.

That happened later in the year when I seized an opportunity for an autumnal camp on Great Mell Fell. I was hoping for footage of dramatic side-lighting and long shadows on the walls and trees looking over Matterdale in the direction of Ullswater. From Great Mell, Catstycam protrudes a little forward of Helvellyn, and in autumn it catches the last light as the sun sets. My intended shot – of that year-end side-light – didn't work out, unfortunately, because cloud rolled in from the west and blocked the sun. Once the sun had set, however, the cloud lifted and the sky turned an array of colours. Thinking on my feet, I set up the camera to capture shots of a lone tree on the fellside silhouetted by a ribbon-blaze of orange and pink. Dawn, again, was fantastic. The freezing night had left everything white with hoar frost. As the sun rose, the side-lighting was perfect. It was one of those days when any number of hours of planning would have delivered nothing; it all came down to luck.

I set up the camera to capture shots of a lone tree on the fellside silhouetted by a ribbon-blaze of orange and pink.

▶ **Lone tree silhouette on Great Mell Fell.**

To the frozen north

The Lake District landscape has changed dramatically over millions of years. The mountains at its heart are the remains of long-extinct volcanoes; the cliffs and corries, crags and valleys carved by the glaciers of successive ice ages. Only recently, in the last few thousand years, has humankind shaped the land with settlements, agriculture and industry.

I wanted *Helvellyn* to feature that story and enlisted the help of Dr Simon Carr, an expert on geology at the University of Cumbria. I'd first met him on a Royal Geographical Society walk from Blencathra Field Centre. He's an eloquent speaker and, yapping over a cuppa afterwards, he'd captivated me by describing the process of geomorphology.

We filmed a scene in Grisedale, and as we were walking out I was grumbling about not being able to afford an animated scene that illustrated the process of ice gouging the rocks. I asked him about locations around the world where the process can still be witnessed and he suggested Iceland. Such an expensive trip was beyond my budget, I told him. Even buying a few seconds of stock footage was too expensive. No problem, he replied; why didn't I accompany him to Iceland the following winter, piggybacking on a trip he was leading with a group studying landscape and climate change?

The eventual trip lasted four days, with another two days of travel, and the footage in *Helvellyn* amounts to no more than two minutes. After Simon introduces the audience to the concept of glaciers in a scene shot in Grisedale, he says: "Where better to get an idea of how the Lakes used to look than ... Iceland?" And we're there, with vast glaciers that are still carving away the volcanic landscape.

The footage demonstrates how Grisedale would have looked 12,000 years ago. From the snowswept wilderness of Iceland, the film transports us back to Helvellyn in winter, the steamer on Ullswater, sheep being fed in the snow; it is, as poet Harriet Fraser calls it, a "land of lives interwoven", where people now work the once ice-barren landscape.

▲ **Striding Edge looking to Ullswater from Lad Crag, Helvellyn.**

◄ **How Grisedale might have looked 12,000 years ago – from the Iceland shoot.**

It is, as poet Harriet Fraser calls it, a "land of lives interwoven", where people now work the once ice-barren landscape.

Fear of flying

The first time I flew was with Matthew Nicholson, the lad I visited the Lake District with as a teenager. He had always wanted to fly – he's a pilot for British Airways these days – but back in the day he was one of the youngest people to fly a hot-air balloon. One summer, when we were 16 or 17, he took me up in one and our flight ended with a crash landing. We only just missed some power lines – we had to bunny-hop over them – and came down in a field full of hay bales, where we were dragged along by the wind, pulling on the rope to release gas, with the bales going *boom, boom, boom* as we hit them. It was the one and only time I've been up in a balloon.

But those hay bales aren't to blame for my fear of flying – it's something more intangible.

On an aeroplane I'm strapped into a seat, looking at a row of heads and a metal door in front. If I'm going to crash and die, I'd rather be able to see exactly where I'm going to crash and die, thank you very much. While travelling, I want to be on terra firma. Give me a bus or a train on the ground where we're meant to be.

Someone once suggested that my fear of flying is down to being a control freak. And there's probably something in that: if I'm in control then anything that goes wrong is my fault – or I'm at least *with* the person who's making the mistake, and can influence them.

My fear of flying doesn't extend to paragliding or being in a microlight, though – neither of which bother me at all. Which is how I ended up filming aerial scenes for *Helvellyn* at 12,000 ft in my friend Matt Lindenberg's light aircraft to get shots that I wouldn't have been able to capture using my drone, which is limited to flying 400 ft above my position on the ground.

In such a small aircraft, I feel secure. If anything goes wrong you can simply glide back down. Besides, my mind's occupied: I have to pay attention as we fly, helping Matt look out for other aircraft and keep a constant eye on possible crash-landing sites (minus hay bales) in case anything does go wrong.

One of the things that surprised me most as I learned more about being airborne was the fact that while drones are limited to flying below 400 ft, the RAF can fly as low as 250 ft.

While out with Matt one day I heard a warning over the radio that the RAF was in the area and would be flying below 7,000 ft for at least an hour. "How the heck are we going to see them when they're flying at 500 mph?" I asked.

"We have a saying in the aviation industry," Matt replied: "the RAF boys will see you before you see them." Which to me translated as: 'Keep your fingers crossed.'"

It really is wing-and-a-prayer stuff.

Spirit of place

You see people from all backgrounds on the fells, each with their own reason for being there, whether it's fitness, hill bagging, adrenaline, soul searching, companionship, nature... Many of us, however, tend to forget about mental health – how being outdoors can be of immense psychological benefit. It is both soul cleansing, and food for the spirit.

Before my bike accident I'd never experienced anything as profound and unsettling as the subsequent depression. I declined the pills the doctors offered me,

> We have a saying in the aviation industry," Matt replied: "the RAF boys will see you before you see them." Which to me translated as: "Keep your fingers crossed." It really is wing-and-a-prayer stuff.

▲ **Adam Convery paragliding over Birkhouse Moor.**

preferring to get outdoors, and I hope I'm able to share some of that message in the film. I'm not afraid to talk about depression, and a specific sequence looks at the positive effects of being outdoors – benefits that can't be achieved using medicine.

It features ambassadors from different mental health organisations, including outdoorsman Alex Staniforth, who has been affected by depression, anxiety and bulimia. I was inspired by how the fells have helped him face those challenges – and how he now shares his message with millions of young people. He's attempted Everest twice, and has climbed all the highest points in the 100 counties of England, Wales, Northern Ireland and Scotland – covering 4,782 miles on foot, by bicycle and kayak.

I always feel better out on the fells, as opposed to being in a town or city. On my first visit to Lakeland, seeing 'God light' shining on Windermere prompted me to think that the world's troubles might be solved if we could bring the world's leaders to wild places. As a species we come from a very different

▶ **Helvellyn massif from the light aircraft shoot.**

environment to the one so many live and work in today. Advances in culture and technology mean we inhabit a world we have not yet evolved to fit. Perhaps being outdoors benefits our mental wellbeing and happiness because it's a reminder of where we came from.

Back on Edge

I had a feeling, after his experience on Sharp Edge in the Blencathra film, that Stuart Maconie might be nervous – perhaps even reluctant – to tackle Striding Edge. But my second shoot with the broadcaster was great fun, thanks in part to the banter on the day.

Five of us were out with him for the shoot: Cumbria Uni apprentices Paul Bacon and Nathan Buckley, old friend David Powell-Thompson, drone pilot Tom Jacobs of Orbital Filming and myself. Between us we managed to convince Maconie that Striding Edge is not Sharp Edge; that it's considered a walk, and that the worst bits can be avoided. Which is mostly true. And fair play to him, he tackled all of it in the end.

I'd envisaged a particular scene, which I explained to him beforehand. The film would show an epic aerial shot of Striding Edge, after which, in a tight edit, we would see David walk past the camera. Then Stuart would stop, look at the ridge ahead and say: "Oh no, not again," before the drone rose from behind him to reveal the full length of the arête and Helvellyn behind. It was one of those rare carefully stage-managed sequences that worked out exactly as planned.

As well as the excitement of the scramble, the sequence also had a sentimental strand. Helvellyn was the first big Lakeland mountain David climbed when he was seven or eight years old. At the summit his dad picked him up and stood him on top of the trig point. I thought including the story would end the scene in a moving way, and as they were walking towards the trig pillar, Maconie surprised us all by asking David: "So, are you going to get up there again?"

> Helvellyn was the first big Lakeland mountain David climbed when he was seven or eight years old. His dad picked him up and stood him on top of the summit trig point.

As David clambered atop the trig point Maconie said: "Well, it was only 20 years ago, you can do it again." It's a subtle dig at the fact that David is not as young as he looks – in fact it was more than 60 years since he last stood on the same spot.

The blend of humour and visual drama worked well. I wanted the film to cover a lot of ground, so I had to edit many sequences and drop some altogether, but this scene remains pretty much intact. It's all about the flow, the connection, and maintaining an all-important emotional heartbeat.

Mr deer herd and other animals

In October 2019 my wingman Nathan and I had a fabulous day filming native red deer in the wilds of the Eastern Fells. I've no idea how nature photographers work on such subjects – I just did my own thing.

The Martindale deer herd is one of the last genetically pure native herds in England. Red deer are two-a-penny in Scotland, but in England the species' bloodline has largely been diluted through interbreeding with the invasive sika, introduced to England in the 19th century. That makes the reds in and around Martindale a special feature of the Lake District.

◀ **Dawn breaks on Striding Edge.**

Until we did the shoot, one deer had seemed much like any other to me. I'd never seen their true colours before. But three days in their presence – watching them wander the landscape, red-orange coats shining in the sunlight – transformed my impression of them.

At a family wedding down south shortly after the shoot I talked to a photographer about how tricky we'd found shooting the annual rut.

He didn't get it: "It's easy," he said.

And perhaps it was for him: he drives around Richmond Park, pokes a camera out of the window and clicks away.

The Martindale herd, however, is wild. The deer live in the mountains and wander free for miles among the Eastern Fells; filming them is the real deal. Nathan and I had to stalk them like hunters for hours, learning their personalities and characters, working out where they liked to spend time. We constantly had to adapt and move accordingly.

Nathan is a student at Cumbria University, one of two apprenticed to me during the time I was making *Helvellyn*. While stalking, he and I worked in tandem – one of us up front, one behind – spreading out, operating stealthily so that we didn't startle the deer or give the herd a reason to bolt. Ideally, the deer would assume we were part of the landscape – fellside wanderers like sheep. If we moved, we moved away from or parallel to them. We applied a kind of deer psychology, too: what were they thinking? we wondered; what would we be concerned about if we were them? We communicated with each other using hand signals.

The star of the show was a grazing stag. When we came upon him – sitting on the moor, munching grass – I indicated to Nathan that he should stay put while I went off to one side. "Stay there and keep filming," I signalled – if the deer was to rise to its feet and run, Nathan would get a parting shot. Avoiding the stag's line of sight, I moved closer, using trees for cover. I secreted myself behind a rowan and set up the tripod. Occasionally I made a deliberate hushed noise, enough to say: "I'm here, I mean no harm."

As the stag grazed I captured footage, and after a couple of minutes I beckoned to Nathan that I intended to move on to the next tree, but he signalled in earnest: "Hold, hold, hold!"

"Why?"

I looked up. The stag had risen and was walking towards me. "Oh blimey, here we go!" The camera rolled as the stag came within 20 feet of me and eyed this hillside intruder. There was no alarm in his gait; I realised he trusted me. He knew, somehow, that I was not there for harm. So I continued to film, utterly focussed on the camera.

Animals seem to trust me. As I continued gathering footage of *Helvellyn*, I found that I could get close to red squirrels, for example, by lying flat on the ground and slowly wiggling over to them, closer and closer. One time I was struggling to get shots of a red squirrel, squinting through the viewfinder unable to work out why the shot wasn't in focus. I thought the autofocus must've failed, but it hadn't – I'd unwittingly got too close for the focus to even operate. The squirrel didn't bat an eyelid, behaving instead like a pet. Those shots are in *Helvellyn*. The squirrel's face fills the cinema screen and if you look closely you can make out my reflection in its eyeball.

As we walked back to Nathan's car after shooting the red deer he told me he'd found the stag encounter a spiritual experience. He pointed out that no-one but us would have a clue about the number of hours we'd spent gathering the shots. And he's right: the deer only feature for a handful of seconds in the film.

But sometimes it's not the shot itself that's special; it's the experience of capturing it.

Sometimes it's not the shot itself that's special; it's the experience of capturing it.

Far from the madding crowd

"How many times have you been up Helvellyn, Terry?" It's a question I've regularly been asked when making the film. My answer surprises some: "Not as many times as you might think."

I have been on the fell frequently, of course, but I've been up others many more times. The reason? Helvellyn is the film's subject, so I want to be looking *at it* rather than *from it*. I constantly seek unique viewpoints and vantage points from which to shoot my subject, and this has taken me to fells typically only traversed by Wainwright-baggers and fell runners.

For example, I've filmed Helvellyn from Bonscale Pike on the east side of Ullswater. When I mention the Pike to others the reply is often: "Oh, never been up there." Yet it has a nice little cairn and a terrific view over Hallin Fell and Place Fell to Helvellyn.

I've had similar conversations about Askham Fell.

Even on bank holiday weekends I've had Askham Fell to myself and the skylarks. People are around, but they're all on the Ullswater Way, visiting the Cock Pit stone circle then Arthur's

▲ **Red squirrel and Martindale stag.**

► **Winter sunset, Pooley Bridge.**

▲
Break in the clouds over Glenridding.

Pike before heading to Howtown, bypassing the best views. Easy Askham Fell offers a sense of wilderness and of being in tune with nature – there are deer, fell ponies, sometimes Galloway cattle – and the views to Helvellyn are exquisite.

The name 'Helvellyn' applies only to that pimple in the middle of the massif that happens to be the highest point. When you see it from the air you can appreciate that the fell top itself is part of a huge range. In the film, climber Simon Yates is depicted going up the ridge of Nethermost Pike, demonstrating that off-the-beaten-track routes onto Helvellyn are exciting and different. I hope the film encourages people to seek out different routes and explore the massif more widely.

While I love sharing these quieter locations, there are some I choose not to broadcast because I don't want them overwhelmed by visitors. I haven't disclosed, for example, the location of Wordsworth's eponymous daffodils on the shores of Ullswater. Most visitors believe they're at Aira Force, but the flowers there are not of the native variety – they're Dutch, planted some time in the past and now invasive.

For the love of Friends

If you'd told me four years ago that I would one day become a patron of the campaigning charity Friends of the Lake District (Friends, or FLD), I would've laughed. While I've always had a passing interest in the politics of conservation, I tend to live in my own little world, outside of the bigger picture.

But I like what Friends stands for; it's supported by members who have a genuine love for the Lake District.

My first taste of conservation politics came when I was asked to become a patron for Nurture Lakeland. At the time, I believed the organisation was conservation-orientated, but it gradually became apparent – to me, at least – that its main focus lay elsewhere, in representing not the Lakeland landscape, but business interests.

Less than a year after I joined, the organisation rebranded itself as the Lake District Foundation and I, as a patron, was invited to talk at its relaunch. The group had failed to speak out against recent proposals to string zip-wires across Thirlmere reservoir – a scheme I strongly believed went against everything a national park should stand for – and when I was asked not to denounce it during the event I felt I had no choice but to resign, and do so publicly, in protest. I followed my heart and, shaking with nerves, said my piece to the audience before bolting to the bar. Which was shut.

Was I right to speak out? I worried that making enemies in high places could damage my burgeoning career, but I didn't need to worry for long: the feedback I received from the public was overwhelmingly positive. People, it seemed, wanted me to speak out on issues that affected the landscapes they loved.

The Thirlmere zip-wire was just one of several proposed developments threatening the Lake District. Plans for gondolas, houseboats and tarmacked cycle paths have more in common with theme parks than a national park. And there are some in the Lake District National Park Authority who seem more concerned with commercialising the area's great asset – its landscape – and boosting visitor numbers than conserving and protecting the area.

FLD and I are kindred spirits, both moved by the landscape to defend it from inappropriate and unsustainable development. Some accuse us of being resistant to change. The charge is misplaced; what few detractors acknowledge is the charity's work on cultural heritage projects and nature restoration, building dry-stone walls, planting trees and wildflowers, conserving wildlife, working with youth groups and schools to get kids outdoors.

One of the celebratory messages in *Helvellyn*

▲ **Terry with campaigners from Friends of the Lake District and Rosthwaite residents at a rally on Latrigg.** © Andrew Locking.

> There are some in the Lake District National Park Authority who seem more concerned with commercialising the area's great asset – its landscape – and boosting visitor numbers than conserving and protecting the area.

◀
Helvellyn and its Edges.

▶
First light hits a distant Helvellyn above Ullswater.

is that successive generations care deeply about nature and the environment. Momentum is building behind the concerns of our age, typified by the likes of Amy Bray, the teenage Cumbrian conservationist whose 'Another Way' movement is spreading awareness of climate change and environmental concerns. Amy brings her message to *Helvellyn* in a short but important statement about what the mountain means to her generation, and how a love for the landscape has inspired her to fight for the environment.

In another scene, kids are pictured learning bush craft skills in the woods above Lower Bridge End Farm in St John's in the Vale. One of them comments that he doesn't see things like sticks at home, and says the view down the lake makes him want to spend more time outdoors. He even asked, off-camera, if he could stay the night in the woods. To young people like him, landscapes offer nourishment for the soul.

Over the past decade, while producing *Life of a Mountain*, I've seen an increasing number of visitors of all ages and backgrounds taking to the fells. I've never seen so many young people exploring, and it warms my heart to see how much the next generation cares about nature, the environment and the experiences the Lake District has to offer. In contrast, it's been heartbreaking to witness the barrage of commercial threats facing the national park.

> It warms my heart to see how much the next generation cares about nature, the environment and the experiences the Lake District has to offer.

Some say offcomers like me should stay out of the ever-noisier debate around development; that locals know best. But it was offcomers like Beatrix Potter who helped save much of this treasured landscape from industrial threats, and offcomers like Alfred Wainwright who chronicled the area's beauty.

I owe my career to this special landscape, to the unrivalled intimacy and beauty that has inspired countless artists, writers, photographers, poets and film makers.

Born 86 years ago, Friends was one of the driving forces behind the designation and protection of the area that I love more than anywhere else in the world – the Lake District National Park – which is, first and foremost, a people's Park.

A sunrise shared

In late November, 2019, Sue had a day or two off work. I'd been planning a winter camp to capture dawn footage of freezing fog spilling across Ullswater and lapping around Helvellyn. Sue, however, persuaded me to stay at home with her instead. I agreed, on condition that she let me drag her out next day on a dawn raid up Little Mell Fell, one of my favourite vantage points. "We'll have to be up at half-five," I warned her, "and out of the door at half-six." It was set to be a luxurious day out for me – with Sue as my private chauffeur.

It was bitterly cold next day as we started up Little Mell Fell in fog, but the air warmed as we climbed above the inversion. Sue had never experienced conditions like it before and, other than the cold, she loved it. We watched the sun rise over Arthur's Pike and Loadpot Hill; and we watched as first Helvellyn then Ullswater lit up. Catstycam looked magical under a thick

white frost bathed in golden sunlight. Such mornings are what drive me to get up in the early hours, no matter how tired I am. They offer experiences no amount of money can buy.

We returned home to warm up, and when Sue nodded off in the afternoon I took the opportunity to sneak into the Pennines, up Great Dun Fell, to get shots across the inversion – which had hung around all day – to Helvellyn. The sun was, however, by then too bright and the air too hazy for clear images, so I returned home. I was tired myself by now, but also a little frustrated that I'd failed to get my hoped-for footage. Looking out, I realised the fog – a thick, freezing fog – was lingering and seemed likely to stay beyond sunset. So I jumped onto my bike and headed out for a third time, back up Dun Fell. As the sun dipped in the southwest, the silhouettes of Helvellyn and the Eastern Fells rose clear against an orange horizon, golden clouds rolling down the valley like waves. I stood entranced as the camera rolled, footage nailed.

If Sue hadn't talked me out of camping the previous night I would've missed out on these rare sunset shots of mist over the Eden Valley, Helvellyn looming large beyond. I went to bed a happy man.

'Lives interwoven'

'In Our Hands' is a poem written by Harriet Fraser to mark the 85th anniversary of Friends of the Lake District. It was the idea of Ruth Kirk, Friends' landscape engagement officer, to capture the essence of the Lake District in a poem that would inspire and act as a call to action to look after the land around us. It is a celebration of the roots and reasons why charities like Friends exist.

When approached by Friends, the initial idea was that my students Paul and Nathan would produce the video. We bounced ideas around about having members of the public recite the words, but their plan was to have voice-overs accompanying fellscape scenes. I had a different vision. "We need every person who reads a line to be seen on camera," I said, "and seen doing different things around the Lake District. We need the fell runner, the farmer, the swimmer... We need people of all ages and backgrounds."

I left the students to it, but when the first couple of shoots didn't work out I took charge. Time-wise it didn't matter because at that point I was ahead of schedule on *Helvellyn*. So we hammered the Friends shoot for three months, getting a multitude of shots, which I then edited into a final film – a kind of visual poem. When it was finished I decided I wanted to include it in *Helvellyn* because it represents the voices of people who love Lakeland. Thankfully, Harriet is not burdened by an ego and didn't mind the public speaking her lines. She didn't even mind that I'd changed one or two – some inadvertently – for the context of the film.

The poem conveys an important message – one that transcends politics – regarding our connection to landscapes. It plays an important role in *Helvellyn*. Each line of poetry is read by a different person – around 30 in total – with a connection to Lakeland. I even make an Alfred Hitchcock-style cameo appearance, reciting a line myself while wild camping with my camera, which I think encapsulates what I'm all about.

'In Our Hands' premièred before an audience on the big screen at Rheged and I took the opportunity to surprise them with a 50-odd-minute sample of footage from *Helvellyn*. Watching the material in the cinema for the first time, I felt detached – as though I was watching someone else's film – and for the first time I got an inkling of the interest building in the still-incomplete documentary. "Bloody hell, Terry, you've knocked it out of the park," I was told. One kind person called it: "A masterpiece in the making".

Paul, Nathan and I were punching the air – it was a huge morale boost and in the bar afterwards I sat down, knackered, and smiled. "It works," I thought, "all our hard work is paying off".

Pre-screenings like this are no excuse to get complacent, though. I took plenty of lessons from it: little things, such as what made the audience laugh, and what should have made them laugh but didn't; I also realised that some scenes I'd had in mind to edit didn't need any more work doing to them.

▲ **University of Cumbria student apprentice Paul Bacon prepares to film on Hallin Fell.**

As the sun dipped in the southwest, the silhouettes of the Eastern Fells rose clear against an orange horizon, golden clouds rolling down the valley like waves.

◀ **Summer dawn from an overnight bivouac on Sheffield Pike.**

Most of all, I realised I had to maintain the building momentum. I thought of all the autumn and winter footage I still had to bag. "I can't just leave it like that – I need to end on a proper high!"

That's one reason why I've pushed myself so hard on *Helvellyn*: it's not just about others' expectations – it's my own expectations of bringing that whole *Life of a Mountain* journey to a satisfying end; and making everyone who has known and supported me through the years proud.

It's not over 'til the last cut's made.

Professor Terry

The University of Cumbria is one of the sponsors of *Life of a Mountain: Helvellyn*. When I was invited to a meeting in Ambleside in mid-December 2019 with vice chancellor Julie Mennell I assumed I was going to be asked to update her on progress, chat about my student apprentices and show her a few short edits. I hoped I might even be able to ask for a little more money to help finish the film.

I arrived in Ambleside to find that campus director Dr Lois Mansfield was also to sit in on the meeting. I like Lois – she's sound as a pound and appears in *Helvellyn* wearing her other hat as Professor of Upland Landscapes. As we waited for Julie to arrive we had a catch-up, during which I mentioned I might ask Julie for more money. Lois smiled, which I interpreted as: "Fat chance!" In retrospect, however, she knew what was coming.

When Julie arrived, she offered me the post of Professor of Practice.

I was dumbstruck. I felt overwhelmed that the university thought so highly of me. Based in the Ambleside campus, the work would involve teaching aspects of the arts, photography and outdoor film, she told me. I was also to produce bite-size videos to promote courses on social media. Julie explained that my appointment was part of the university's possible plan to relocate some of their media courses – including Wildlife Media, the course on which Paul and Nathan were studying – from its Carlisle campus to Ambleside; something for which I had been arguing.

Sue noted the tears in my eyes – tears that stretched back to the death of my grandparents.

I received a lovely email from Lois afterwards saying it was the first time she'd seen me lost for words.

I was still trying to process the news hours later, and when it finally sunk in Sue noted the tears in my eyes – tears that stretched back to the death of my grandparents and the subsequent years that derailed my studies and my own chance of going to uni.

▶ **Filming from a frosty Helvellyn wild camp.** © David Forster.

A sudden gust of wind

In late February, when I was trying to squeeze a sequence of shots into a period when the fells were in fine winter conditions, I suffered an injury at Red Tarn that saw me back in hospital.

Paul, Nathan and I had been filming father and son Charlie and Isaac Sproson skiing down Helvellyn.

I wanted to include an adrenaline sequence with a human element, so I got in touch with the Lake District Ski Club, which operates the low-key ski tow on Raise in the Helvellyn range. It's a unique facility in that skiers have to walk in to reach it carrying all their gear, unlike the ski developments in Scotland, which tend to be eyesores with car parks and restaurants. That light footprint ties in nicely with several of the film's conservation messages; indeed, the ski tow is so unobtrusive that for a long time, I – like, I suspect, many fell-walkers – was unaware it was even there.

To follow the scene about the club's history, I wanted action. I remember seeing newspaper reports about people skiing down Helvellyn's rugged eastern face. "What nutters do that?" I wondered at the time: the slope towards Red Tarn, I've been told, is 45° in places – a serious undertaking. I put word out that I wanted to film someone skiing down it, which led me to mountain guide Charlie Sproson, who lives at Greenside Mines with his Nordic-walking guide wife Nicky and their son Isaac. Helvellyn is their sprawling back yard – there's not an inch of it they don't know.

Isaac, 16, is a proficient skier and it was he who volunteered himself and his dad for the roles. Recent storms meant we had to monitor snow conditions before anything could happen: it had to be perfect for skiing – powdery and without risk of avalanche. We kept an eye on the forecast while Charlie checked conditions during regular fell runs. Between us we worked out the best day, which came in late February after a succession of freeze-thaws had helped consolidate the snow pack.

▲
"Which nutters do that?" Isaac Sproson and dad Charlie, captured with a GoPro.

◀
Heather sunburst, Ullswater.

> I remember seeing newspaper reports about people skiing down Helvellyn's rugged eastern face. "What nutters do that?" I wondered at the time.

We set up base for the day in the bowl alongside Red Tarn. I worked out where I wanted the low-level cameras sited to follow the action from afar, then attached GoPros to harnesses worn by Charlie and Isaac. Initially they were forward-facing, so that the skis and poles were visible. For the second run I swapped the harnesses around so they captured the skier following behind. Finally, we had a camera attached to a drone, which was capturing the action from above. I had wanted to film them tipping over the edge from the summit, but the cornice was too large to get close enough. That meant making compromises, though I was more than happy with the dramatic footage we were getting. If I was to ever fulfil my dream of shooting a *James Bond* scene, this was the time...

Winds gusting over the edge at between 50 and 60 mph made conditions tough for the skiers, especially when they had to slog back up through snow on Swirral Edge for the next run: the skis, strapped to their backs, acted like sails, catching the downwinds.

After the second run we were gathered at basecamp to prepare for the next sequence when a sudden gust of wind enveloped us. Kit flew everywhere and I leapt to grab Tom's drone. As the wind spun its propellers, the blades clipped one of the fingers on my left hand.

For a few seconds I thought nothing of it – my hands were numb with cold as I'd had my gloves off to control a camera – and I merely thought: "That's gonna hurt in the morning." Twenty seconds later, blood was spraying the snow red. Because of the blood I couldn't tell what damage had been done, so I stuck my finger into the snow, hoping to stem the flow. Get a tight dressing on, I thought, and I'll be fine. But an hour or so later, after a couple more takes, I was feeling unwell and knew Penrith Urgent Treatment Centre would be getting a visit.

When we arrived, the field dressing was removed to reveal my finger, still frozen from three hours earlier, turning black. The colour returned slowly as it warmed, but that was when the pain kicked in. The propeller had sliced through my finger just below the first joint, breaking the bone. The fingertip and nail were hanging by a sliver of flesh. The wound was bound, dressed and splinted, and I was told it would heal well if I took care of it. If it healed as well as the other fingers on my left hand, I said – which had nearly all been broken at one time or another – I'd be satisfied. It would, however, take weeks and I was told not to get the dressing wet. I'm left-handed, so I couldn't use some of the buttons on my camera, or grip the handlebar on my bike properly. It was frustrating, especially because I had yet to film scenes with paragliders on Helvellyn, and with the Ordnance Survey.

There was good news to end the day, though: coming out of hospital I checked my phone to find an email from the BBC asking how *Helvellyn* was progressing. Trying to type a reply was not easy.

> *Scafell Pike* was a moment in time that I was able to seize. I had a vision and followed it. The technology – affordable cameras, social media, online fundraising – enabled me to achieve something that would have been impossible even five years earlier.

End in sight

Like the premières for *Scafell Pike* and *Blencathra*, *Helvellyn* is set to debut at Rheged in May. I'm not superstitious; I've chosen the month purely for sentimental reasons.

I haven't read the small print in the contract. All I know is that Rheged insists I'm there from half-past-four.

I'll probably shed a tear when the curtain falls on the final film, but a big part of me will also be thinking: "Thank heavens it's over." I need a rest from looking at webcams and satellite images on my phone at three in the morning and then deciding whether to go out filming. I need to switch off and have a break. Most of all, I'd like to enjoy the fells as a normal human being again.

Alfred Wainwright said that his guidebooks, as well as being his legacy, were there to remind him of his time on the fells in old age. That's how I feel about *Life of a Mountain*. Hopefully, when I'm older I'll return to watch them, to transport me back to the fells I've come to call home.

Life of a Mountain has been a case of 'cometh the hour, cometh the man'. *Scafell Pike* was a moment in time that I was able to seize. I had a vision and followed it. The technology – affordable cameras, social media, online fundraising websites – enabled me to achieve something that would have been impossible even five years earlier. Each film has been a journey, and the results are my reward for the graft and suffering. I've been lucky to pull the films off, and even luckier that they've captured the imaginations of people locally, nationally and worldwide.

Helvellyn will be the film that defines the trilogy, that not only brings this stage of my life to a close, but also takes my visual tribute to the fells to another level. *Life of a Mountain: Scafell Pike* will always be special to me because it was the first, and some will undoubtedly prefer its raw, rough edges.

But *Helvellyn* will not disappoint. I've put my heart and soul into it and pulled out all the stops to ensure it blows the audience's socks off. It's a grand finale.

▶ **Morning light over Glenridding and Patterdale.**

◀
Ullswater from the Helvellyn summit trig point.

Parting shot

I returned home knackered after an overnight camp on Great Mell Fell, where I'd captured shots at sunset and dawn. At just 1,762 ft Great Mell is no Lakeland giant, but it had been a physically exhausting few weeks and my pack seemed to be getting heavier and heavier.

I checked the forecast and saw it was looking good for dawn the following day.

When I told Sue she insisted I'd done too much and should stay in and rest. Deep inside, however, I reckoned I'd be fine. With a few pints and some food in my belly I'd be asleep in front of the fire by eight, then out of the house by four the next morning.

True to form, my body clock woke me at half-three. I considered plans for the day over coffee. Would Askham Fell or Dun Fell offer the best location? When I made my mind up I let Sue know, waking her gently with a kiss on the cheek to tell her I was going out.

"You're not, are you? You need to sleep."

I pulled the curtains back an inch. Stars blazed above the Eden dark.

I thought back to the words of my grandmother – "Make the most of your life, Terry" – that had been spoken a lifetime ago.

I've never wanted to look back when I'm an old man and regret the things I didn't do – to think: "I wish I'd gone out that morning; I wish I'd pushed more."

I thought back to the words of my grandmother – "Make the most of your life, Terry" – that had been spoken a lifetime ago.

Then I looked back at Sue: "I'm going out, darling – there'll be plenty of time to sleep."

Kit

SCAFELL PIKE

Video camera:
Panasonic AG-AC90

DSLR:
Canon 600D with Tamron 10–24mm f3.5 lens and kit lens

Sound:
TASCAM DR-40 unit with RODE tie-clip microphone
TASCAM DR-60D MKII unit with RODE NTG2 with Blimp and Deadcat windshields

BLENCATHRA

Video cameras:
Sony A7S MK1 with Metabones lens adaptor and Canon L-Series 24–105mm lens
Sony PXW-X70 with microphone and Rycote Softie

DSLR:
Canon 600D with Tamron 10–24mm f3.5 lens and kit lens
Canon 6D

Sound:
2 x Zoom H1 recorders with Rode lapel microphones
TASCAM DR-40 unit with RODE tie-clip microphone
TASCAM DR-60D MKII unit with RODE NTG2 with Blimp and Deadcat windshields

Aerial footage filmed by Flying Glass:
DJI Phantom and DJI Matrice with Sony FS7 and relevant lenses

Other equipment:
Syrp Genie and Magic Carpet slider

HELVELLYN

Video cameras:
Sony A7S MK1 with Metabones lens adaptor and Canon L-Series 24–105mm lens
Sony PXW-X70 with microphone and Rycote Softie
GoPro HERO7 plus accessories

DSLR:
Canon 600D with Tamron 10–24mm f3.5 lens and kit lens
Canon 6D with Tamron 150–600mm G2 lens and Tamron 90mm Macro lens

Sound:
2 x Zoom H1 recorders with Rode lapel microphones
TASCAM DR-60D MKII unit with RODE NTG2 with Blimp and Deadcat windshields

Aerial footage filmed by Orbital Filming:
DJI Mavic Pro

Additional aerial filming by Terry Abraham:
Sony PXW-X70 from fixed-wing aircraft flown up to 12,000 ft

Other equipment:
Syrp Genie and Magic Carpet slider

All films edited in Vegas Pro

Time-lapse sequences processed in Adobe Lightroom

94%
REC
07:55:39:04
79min
XAVC
PEAKING
PPS
F6.8
0dB
50
CH1
CH2